GW01605855

MURDER IN OLD BERKSHIRE

TYBURN. (MC)

MURDER IN OLD BERKSHIRE

A collection of sudden deaths in and around the old county

by

ROGER LONG

Barracuda Books Limited
Buckingham, England

MCMCX

PUBLISHED BY BARRACUDA BOOKS LIMITED
BUCKINGHAM, ENGLAND
AND PRINTED BY
REDWOOD PRESS LIMITED
WILTSHIRE, ENGLAND

BOUND BY
HUNTER & FOULIS LIMITED
EDINBURGH, SCOTLAND

JACKETS PRINTED BY
CHENEY & SONS LIMITED
BANBURY, OXON

LITHOGRAPHY BY
FORE COLOUR GRAPHICS LIMITED
HERTFORD, ENGLAND

TYPESET BY
PHOENIX MANOR
BLETCHLEY, ENGLAND

© Roger Long 1990

All rights reserved. No part of this publication may be reproduced, stored in a retrieval system, or transmitted, in any form or by any means, electronic, mechanical, photocopying, recording or otherwise, without the prior permission of Barraduca Books Limited.

Any copy of this book issued by the Publisher as clothbound or as a paperback is sold subject to the condition that it shall not by way of trade or otherwise, be lent, re-sold, hired out or otherwise circulated without the Publisher's prior consent, in any form of binding or cover other than that in which is is published, and without a similar condition including this condition being imposed on a subsequent

CONTENTS

TYBURN, WHERE MURDERERS AND MANY OTHERS MET THEIR FATES. HOGARTH'S PICTURE SHOWS THE POPULARITY OF SUCH SPECTACLES. (MC)

INTRODUCTION

Murder is a contradiction: the ultimate act of destruction, almost always for short-term gain — for money, through anger, for love of another, to escape responsibility. From highwaymen to wife-killer, baby farmer to mail robber, the guilty men — and women — achieve lasting notoriety, their crimes recorded in court records and in newspapers.

This anthology of murders in and around the old county of Berkshire includes the villains of Broadmoor, the mass murderer of Colnbrook, Maidenhead's mail robbers, Bisham's heartless lady, and the extraordinary case of the actor and the shopkeeper killed at Reading. There's the Quaker slain at Slough, Wild Will Darrell of Littlecote, the dreadful Mrs Dyer, death on duty at Hungerford and a crime of passion at Clewer. The missing wife of Windsor shared her fate with an unfortunate Watchfield wife, while the Chequers at Harwell witnessed manslaughter as the customers stood by; the spirit of Cumnor recalls an ancient killing, and tragedy touches Touchen End. Wokingham, Caversham, Mapledurham, Lambourn, Coley Park, Blagrave and Combe complete the collection.

Murder in Old Berkshire is a look back at an unusual facet of the county's past, rarely brought to book.

KEY TO CAPTION CREDITS

CB	CLIVE BIRCH
GB	GEOFFREY BAGLEY
BCL	BERKSHIRE COUNTY LIBRARY
MC	THE MANSELL COLLECTION
VDMC	VALE & DOWNLAND MUSEUM CENTRE
TM	THE LATE TOM MIDDLETON
DS	DAVID SCURRELL
PS	PAUL SPICE
RS	RAY SOUTH

CLAUDE DUVAL DANCES ON THE HEATH.

HIGHWAYMEN OF BROADMOOR

The green and pleasant district where the Royal County of Berkshire meets Hampshire and Surrey is an affluent and elegant area. But it was not always like this. What is now a forest in the Wokingham, Bracknell and Camberley triangle was originally part of a great moor, hence the name of its most famous feature, Broadmoor.

The moor was virtually desolate, every tree and bush a landmark, the scant villages a collection of shacks. The inhabitants were morose and suspicious, their occupations of charcoal burning and peat digging supplemented by anything that came their way.

Many major stage routes ran across the moor, connecting London and Windsor with Portsmouth, Southampton, Bath and Bristol, Their passengers braved Hounslow Heath and Maidenhead Thicket, which were infested with highwaymen, before venturing across the moor with its notorious footpads and villains.

Many of the highwaymen became legends. William Davis, known as the 'Golden Farmer' from Gloucester, was apparently respectable, but he subsidised his living by robbing coaches on the moor. Davies had a wife and 18 children, and he supported them in style. He was the most successful of the moor's highwaymen, practising for 42 years until he was spotted by one of his victims in a London street. Caught, tried and sentenced, he was executed in Fleet Street.

The most romantic of the highwaymen was Claude Duval, the son of a respectable miller from Normandy. He came to England in the service of some young travellers, and shortly afterwards became the page of the Duke of Richmond. Realising the far greater financial potential of a life on the road, he took to the moor with resounding success. This way of life in turn afforded Duval many properties in the area. Apart from his large London abode, his nefarious activities brought him a cottage at Lightwater, another at Chobham, a house at Wokingham and one at Sonning.

Chivalrous to a fault, the story of his taking only £100 of the £400 he knew to be aboard a stagecoach at Bagshot, on the condition that an attractive lady passenger would dance with him, is authentic.

When Duval was arrested in London, high society queued to commiserate with him in his cell. He is buried in Covent Garden, and his epitaph reads: 'Here lies Duval. Reader, if male thou art, look to thy purse, if female to thy heart. Much havoc has he made of both.'

Dick Turpin used the moor, but was said not to be fond of it, possibly because of the competition.

Parson Darby, a gentleman of the cloth, would preach the paths of righteousness to his devoted flock by day, and rob London coaches by night. The preacher overstepped the mark when he called the *Royal Mail* to a halt on the moor near Bagshot. The driver urged the horses on and was shot. The parson fled emptyhanded. He was ridden down before he could reach the comparative safety of his parsonage at Yateley.

Darby was captured and gibbeted on the heath close to the scene of his exploits. His body was left to rot as a warning to others who might be tempted to stray from those paths of righteousness. The hamlet of Darby Green was named after the notorious parson.

Apart from these gentlemen, there were others of varying degrees of notoriety. There was Captain Show, a seemingly respectable ex-army man, who plied his trade around the Sunningdale area of the moor. Snows Ride, a local thoroughfare, was in all probability named in his dubious honour. There was also Captain Hawes, another ex-serviceman, who was finally executed for robberies on the moor; Whitney, the butcher, who was feared for his savagery and barbarism; Captain Stafford, a Londoner who found fame on the moor, and Thomas Simpson (Old Mob) who, although hideously ugly, managed to evade capture regularly by disguising himself as a woman.

In the early 18th century, Windsor Forest bordered on Broadmoor and Bagshot Heath. It was mostly Crown land, divided into 'Rayles' (enclosed areas for herding deer). Colonel Negus, a hero who had served in Marlborough's army, was given a seat in Parliament and the custodianship of Bigshot Rayle, which he left to the care of his deputy, Baptist Nunn.

At this time, the Rayles were being plagued by a large gang known as the Wokingham Blacks. Led by a man named William Shorter, the gang had begun as a small group of poachers, their nickname derived from their dark clothing and blacked up faces for nocturnal raids in the forest.

The Wokingham Blacks grew in number and audacity, local sheriffs were met with silence from the locals, many of whom were related to the gang, while others were fed and clothed by them. But all were terrified of retaliation which was swift and vicious. A local magistrate had killed some of the gang's dogs at Bagshot, and returned to find his house on fire. Another magistrate, Sir John Cape of Bramshill, sentenced one of their number in his court, and found acres of his new plantation destroyed. The son of a caretaker who had annoyed them was waylaid by four of them and bludgeoned to death. A local farmer's young son was blasted to death through his open bedroom window at Eversley. Thus they maintained their nefarious existence with impunity.

The Wokingham Blacks grew more confident, but that complacency was to be their undoing. Local gentry and landowners found the gang's exploits so expensive and unremitting that measures had to be taken to apprehend them.

It was pointless to try to catch them on their own ground as their friends were too numerous and their alibis too readily available. Therefore, some of their number had to be enticed away to make them more vulnerable.

The services of the Bow Street Runners were obtained, two of whom, Chalk and Fowler, were selected for their rough countenances. In the guise of travelling labourers they were sent to Wokingham Fair as undercover agents. The amount of money they had to spend made Chalk and Fowler outstanding, and this detail was not lost on three of the gang. Intending to relieve the Runners of their seemingly unending supply of money, three young gang members followed them around the taverns. However, on striking up a conversation, Chalk, a little the worse for drink, became talkative and boastful. Much to the annoyance of the scowling Fowler, Chalk proceeded to divulge the source of their income. He said that they were professional witnesses from London, explaining that, if a prosecution lawyer was having difficulty in obtaining a conviction, he would handsomely reward a witness who would state under oath that he had seen the crime committed.

This practice became quite extensive in the 18th century. Witnesses willing to be paid for their services would parade outside courthouses. They would let lawyers know they were available by having ears of corn or hay protruding from their shoes. Lawyers would tap such men on the shoulder, they would go to a quiet corner and a deal would be made. Hence the derisive name of 'strawshoes' was applied in legal circles to anybody who gave witness for money.

The three young Wokingham Blacks were intoxicated by the thought of easy money and the following week were on their way to a rendezvous in London. Chalk and Fowler had agreed to introduce them to a lawyer in a Holborn tavern. No one mentioned their intentions to their leader, William Shorter.

On entering the tavern, the Wokingham men saw Chalk and Fowler accompanied by an elderly man whom they took to be the lawyer. Chalk greeted them and supplied them with beer but, as they drank, they found themselves looking down the barrels of a dozen pistols! The trap had been baited, set and closed.

Under the persuasion of the Bow Street Runners, information was wrung from them about a meeting of the Wokingham Blacks, and a complete troop of Horse Grenadiers was drafted down to the forest. After a pitched battle, no less than 29 of the gang were arrested. William Shorter, however, remained at large with three of his lieutenants.

Baptist Nunn, the caretaker of Bigshot Rayle and Lodge was receiving threats of extortion from the gang. His horse had been slaughtered and a shotgun had been fired through his window at dead of night. Unable to pay, he was being harrassed by them, but had agreed to a meeting near Crowthorne.

Nunn had heard of the arrests, both at Holborn and at Bracknell, and guessed that Shorter was much demoralised and nervous. He informed the Sheriffs of his planned meeting, and helped lay another trap to make the final arrests.

THE READING AND LONDON COACH PASSES WINDSOR, c1820. (CB)

Shorter and his lieutenants were wary of a trap and had watched the forest lodge near Caesar's Camp for several hours before finally making their rendezvous with Baptist Nunn but, as they entered the building, they were surrounded by a dozen officers who had been lying doggo nearby for many hours. Shorter and his accomplices were arrested without a struggle.

The indictments at Reading Crown Court ranged from poaching to murder. The four ringleaders were sentenced to death on the gibbet and their bodies were hung in chains at various crossroads on the moor. Shorter himselfbwas displayed prominently at the busiest intersection of the moor, Wishmoor Cross, where three counties and four parishes meet.

MEASURED from HYDE PARK CORNER.	LONDON TO BATH.	THROUGH READING, MARLBOROUGH, and DEVIZES.

grounds are beautifully disposed, and ornamented with a profusion of wood and water, which, added to their situation on the margin of the Thames, unite in composing a most charming tout ensemble.

SMALLBURY GREEN. *R. Hope*, Esq.; and a little beyond Smallbury Green, Worton House, Lord *J. Hay;* Worton Lodge, *E. C. Southbrook*, Esq.; and Worton Hall, *H. Cerf*, Esq.

COLNBROOK, 1¾m. beyond, Ditton Park, Lord *Montagu.*

SLOUGH. See Windsor Castle, *His Majesty;* and Eton College. This college was founded by the unfortunate Henry VI., and is advantageously situated in a healthy and fertile valley, near the river Thames, which rolls its pellucid stream at a short distance from the walls, greatly contributing to the beauty of this interesting scene. The institution supports 70 scholars, with officers and assistants; besides which, there are seldom less than 300 gentlemen, sons of the nobility and gentry, who board with the masters, and receive their education at this seminary. The college consists of 2 quadrangles, one appropriated to the school, and the lodging of the masters and scholars; the other contains the apartments of the provost and fellows, and also the library, which is considered one of the finest in Europe: some very valuable drawings, paintings, and oriental manuscripts, are among its curiosities. The chapel is a fine structure, ornamented with large abutments, pinnacles, and embrasures; and is similar, in the disposition of its parts, to that of King's College, Cambridge. —— Near Slough, Burnham Grove, Sir *W. Johnston*, Bart.

MAIDENHEAD. Ives Place, *T. Wilson*, Esq.; and Sir *Wm. Herne;* at Bray, Henden's House, Mrs. *A. M. Trenchard;* Kimbers, *W. Dodwell*, Esq.; Altwood, *C. Sawyer*, Esq.; Bullocks Hatch, *Thomas Athorpe*, Esq.; and Down Place, *H. Harford*, Esq.; at Holyport, *H. Walter*, Esq.; and Philberds, *C. Fuller*, Esq.; at Braywick, Braywick Grove, *W. Atkins*, Esq.; Cannon Hill, Mrs. *E. Law;* and Braywick Lodge, Admiral *West.* This neat edifice stands on a gentle eminence, and commands some delightful views. The prospect on one side is heightened by the town of Maidenhead and the village of Taplow, backed by the noble woods of Cliefden and Hedsor: and on the other side it is rendered truly delightful by the proud Castle of Windsor, and the picturesque forest scenery.

MAIDENHEAD THICKET, at a distance, the spire of Shottesbrook Church; near which is Shottesbrook Park,

From Bath		From London
	Over Hounslow Heath, (enclosed)	
95	*To* * Cranford Bridge ☞	12¼
93½	The Magpies	13¾
92	Longford	15¼
	Cross the river Coln	
90	* Colnbrook, *Bucks.*	17¼
	1½ *m. farther,*	
	☞ {*to Windsor, by Datchet,* 3¼ *m.*	
	London to * *WINDSOR* 22 *m.*	
86¾	* Slough	20½
	☞ {*to Eton* 1½ *m., thence to Windsor, across the river Thames,* ¾ *m.*	
	London to Eton College 22 *m.*	
	London to * *WINDSOR* 22¾ *m.*	
86	* Salt Hill	21¼
	1¾ *m. farther,*	
	To Great Marlow, through Burnham, 8¾ *m.* } ☞	
82	* Maidenhead Bridge	25¼
	Cross the river Thames	
	* *MAIDENHEAD,*	
81¼	*Berkshire*	26
	¾ *m. farther,*	
	To Great Marlow, across the Thames, 5 *m.* } ☞	
	London to * *GREAT MARLOW, Bucks.* 31¼ *m.*	
	Maidenhead Thicket,	
79¼	*Junction of the Road*	28
	To Henley, 7 *m.* ☞	
75¼	Hare Hatch	32
73¼	Twyford, *Wilts.*	34
	Cross the river Loddon	
	1 *m. before Reading,*	
	☞ *to Oakingham* 7 *m.*	
68¼	* *READING, Berks.*	39
	Cross the river Kennet	
	To Henley 8 *m.* } ☞ *To Wallingford* 15¼ *m.* }	
	☞ *to Basingstoke* 16 *m.*	
65¾	Calcot Green	41½
63¾	* Theal	43½
	1 *m. farther,*	
	To Wallingford 13½ *m.* ☞	
62	Jack's Booth	45¼
	2½ *m. farther,*	
	☞ {*to Kingsclere* 7¾ *m.* *to Basingstoke* 10½ *m.*	

and Langley Grove, Mrs. *Buckland.*

SALT HILL. Stoke Park, *J. Penn*, Esq. The mansion, one of the most magnificent residences in this part of the county, consists of a large square centre, and two wings, whose north and south fronts are ornamented by a colonnade: the latter front is 196 feet in length, and its whole interior is occupied by an elegant and valuable library of the best authors. The park is rather flat; but commands some fine views, particularly to the south, whence the eye ranges, over a large sheet of water, to the majestic castle of Windsor, beyond which the forest has a very noble appearance. A neat stone bridge is thrown over a large lake which winds itself round the east side of the building. About 300 yards from the north front of the house, stands a handsome fluted column 68 feet high, surmounted with a colossal statue of Sir Edward Coke, by Rosa. —— Beyond this is Stoke Farm, Lord *Sefton;* and Britwell House, Rev. — *Evans.*

MAIDENHEAD BRIDGE. At Taplow, Taplow House, *Pascoe Grenfell*, Esq.; Berry Hill, Lord *Newry;* Taplow Hill, — *Lucas*, Esq.; and Taplow Lodge, Mrs. *Tunno.* From the bridge see Cliefden, Right Hon. Sir *George Warrender*, Bart.; near which is Formosa Place, the elegant seat of Sir *Samuel Young*, Bart.; Formosa Fishery, *unoccupied;* and Hedsor Lodge, Lord *Boston.* This noble mansion stands on an eminence, and commands a very richly diversified country: the convenient domestic arrangements and internal decorations have rendered it a most desirable and commodious residence. The grounds are formed into high sloping hills and deep valleys, and are ornamented by a well-distributed variety of woods. —— Near the above, Dropmore, Lord *Grenville.*

MAIDENHEAD. *Isaac Pocock*, Esq.; The Elms, Mrs. *Hall;* and The Cottage, — *Atkinson*, Esq.

MAIDENHEAD THICKET. Stubbings, Col. *Brotherton;* at a distance, Hall Place, Sir *Gilbert East*, Bart.; and Bisham Abbey, *Geo. Vansittart*, Esq.

HARE HATCH, 1m. before, Bear Hill, Mrs. *W. Cavendish;* and Bear Place, Sir *Morris Ximines.* This is an elegant modern edifice with wings, pleasantly situated on an elevated spot, in a fine woodland country. The grounds contain a pleasing variety of inequalities, tufted with woods; and the views towards the south and east are extensive and beautiful.

TWYFORD. At a distance, at Shiplake, Rev. — *Howman;* Shiplake House, Dr. *Phillimore;* and Holme Wood, Lord *Mark Ker.*

THE LONDON-BATH ROAD THROUGH MAIDENHEAD THICKET IN PATERSON'S ROADS — THE BIBLE OF THE COACH TRAVELLER, HERE IN THE 1826 18TH EDITION. (CB)

WORKING MODEL OF JARMAN'S EQUIPMENT AT THE OSTRICH.

COLNBROOK'S TILTING BED

The Ostrich Inn still stands in the ancient village of Colnbrook near Slough. The village, now blessedly encircled by a by-pass, was once on the main A4, and before that, on the principal London to Bath stage route.

There is little doubt that some sort of hostelry stood on the site from the Middle Ages. The name 'Ostrich' is in all probability a corruption of hospice. It has records going back to the reign of Henry II in about 1165. The position of the old inn made it attractive to wealthy friends of Royalty, wishing to change their clothes before presenting themselves to the monarch at Windsor.

The Ostrich first came to fame through the nefarious exploits of its one-time landlord, Jarman. It is difficult to put a specific date on when Jarman became 'mine host' at the ancient hostelry; the time of his villainies lies somewhere between the inn's foundation in 1106, and the rebuilding of around 1500.

Thomas Deloney, reckoned to be England's first novelist, mentions dastardly goings-on there in the late 1500s, so the Ostrich has the distinction of being one of the half a dozen claimants to the title of oldest inn in England, and is also the first mentioned in an English novel. Deloney's account of Jarman's crimes has many contradictory elements. He has King Henry I ordering the inn to be burned to the ground in 1130 after Jarman's murders and skulduggery were discovered. This did not happen. Thomas Deloney may have used a little poetic licence to embroider a good yarn.

The rather enigmatic facts are these: Jarman was the landlord of the Ostrich, probably in the 1300s. To supplement his income, he devised an intricate and profitable scheme. He would ply a wealthy traveller with drink until he was besozzled, and then lead the unfortunate traveller up to his best room. When the unsuspecting man was safely ensconced in a deep slumber, Jarman would pull two bolts from the floor below, and the bed, which was screwed to the floor, would tip up to a 45° angle, sliding the poor wayfarer into a great vat of boiling fat strategically placed below. The victim was drowned and boiled to death at the same time. While the pain must have been excruciating, death was almost certainly instantaneous.

Jarman would then take the man's belongings, deposit the body in a nearby river and sell his horse and clothes to the taciturn gypsies that wandered the moor.

Jarman, it would seem, enjoyed the rewards of his lucrative endeavours for many years. It is not known exactly how he was caught, but there are several theories. One is that the small river or stream was low one night as it was a particularly dry period, the innkeeper deposited the body as per usual, but by the morning it had not drifted away. It was found by some local horsemen and this was the beginning of the end for the murderous publican. This theory also has the last unfortunate victim as a man called Coln, hence the name Colnbrook.

THE OSTRICH INN, COLNBROOK.

Another theory suggests that an intended victim was at his chamber pot, relieving himself after vast quantities of ale, and turned around in time to see his bed at a perilous angle. He ran to the door in his nightshirt, raising the alarm.

Yet another story tells of a young ostler who worked at the inn. The lad heard curses and hollering coming from the kitchen and, on entering the kitchen discovered the victim feet up in the vat, and Jarman cursing in pain and rubbing spattered fat from his face.

It will never be known how Jarman was caught, but caught he was, and condemned to hang. Hanging would seem quite a lenient sentence considering the enormity of his crime in those harsh old days. On the scaffold an unrepentant Jarman boasted of some sixty or seventy murders. He no doubt thought 'If you've got to go, go in style'. A nearer estimate of his victims would be between fifteen and twenty.

NEWGATE PRISON — ABOVE: THE CHAPEL AND BIRD CAGE WALK, WHERE MURDERERS WERE BURIED; BELOW: THE FLOGGING WARD AND THE CHAIN CUPBOARD. (PS)

THE 1780 MAIDENHEAD AND MARLOW POST COACH. (TM)

SOHO SQUARE IN THE 1780s, WHERE THE WESTON BROTHERS WERE CAUGHT.

The Great Maidenhead Mail Robbery

On a bitterly cold night in 1781, two young brothers waited to rob the *Royal Mail*. They stamped their feet and flapped their arms around their bodies to try to keep out the extreme chill. Both men had a history of lawlessness, petty felonies and misdemeanours, but this was to be their first foray into serious and hopefully prosperous crime, an opportunity prompted by pure chance.

George Weston was 29 years of age, his brother Joseph some six years younger. George was much as the wanted posters described him: 5′7″ tall, thickset, ruddy complexioned, and with the appearance of a country farmer. His distinguishing marks were a duelling scar across his hand, and also a deformed thumb that had been broken and badly reset; it gave the impression of a parrot's bill.

Joseph Weston, at 23, was some 2″ taller than his brother, fair haired, smooth complexioned with a genteel bearing and a refined attitude.

It was now nearly two in the morning and the two young men were awaiting their prey. The *Royal Mail* generally evokes in the reader's mind an image of a coachman with horn, and an armed guard, dashing through the night behind a team of six or more lathered horses. In 1781, when coaching was in its infancy, this was far from the case. The frost-bitten Weston brothers were waiting just off the Bath Road near Maidenhead in Berkshire. The *Bristol Mail* was heading towards them at the piteously slow speed of a horse and cart, urged forward by a sleep-weary teenage post-boy.

The brothers waited in anticipation.

The Westons' brief life stories would have done credit to the swashbuckling imagination of a Stevenson, Scott or Dumas. They were born in Staffordshire to a local farmer. A well-respected man in the community, he made sure that the boys were well educated and also conversant with practical methods of making a living.

George became a proficient scholar with an aptitute for mathematics. As soon as he was of age he took himself off to London to work as a merchant's clerk. His natural ability with figures soon earned him promotion to a trusted position, where he became responsible for most of the financial undertakings of the firm. It was not long before he had found a position in the same firm for young Joseph, as a junior clerk. The brothers enjoyed the hedonistic pleasures of the big city's pleasures that did not come cheaply.

George found that his position enabled him to divert a little of the firm's money into his own pocket. It was virtually undetectable. As time passed, however, an excess of gambling, drinking and womanising got the brothers into more debt than George's dexterous manipulations could possibly conceal.

The bubble was about to burst.

One morning the constables arrived, but the birds had flown, and they found the offices empty. The brothers were sailing from Dover *en route* to Amsterdam.

George and Joseph found the law in Holland a little too efficient for their fraudulent undertakings. They were also handicapped as conmen by not being able to master the language so, after a few months, they landed back in England with altered names and appearances. There they decided to go their separate ways and were not to join forces again for another three years.

George attempted a nearly honest living as a part-time thespian, and also as a tutor to the children of wealthy clients. Neither profession yielded sufficient funds for his expensive lifestyle. He supplemented his income by petty thieving from his pupils' parents, and also by a touch of blackmail, often finding his benefactors had been slightly compromised with the serving staff.

George Weston exhibited style and imitated respectability. It was also reported that he had the audacity to join the Special Constables, but all pretence was blown asunder when he was noticed pawning stolen articles by a fellow officer. George took to the hills and went to seek solace with his younger brother.

He found Joseph in the Hungerford area, where he had rented a small farm. He was making a lucrative living rustling horses, cattle and sheep from the surrounding farms by night, and then selling them in the Newbury and Marlborough markets by day.

Profitable as the business was, the brothers knew it had a limited lifespan. They hankered for the bright lights of the capital, so in early 1778 they sold up and headed once again for London.

George took over from young Joseph as the main provider. Bills of exchange, the forerunners of cheques, were just coming into fashion. At first they were quite crude and it took little skill and expertise to forge the signature, and then fraudulently put them to financial advantage.

The brothers' opulent and sybaritic lifestyle soon made them take chances. It was not long before they were fleeing again, this time from the Bow Street Runners.

Residents of Horncastle, Lincoln and Boston were the next to suffer their nefarious practices, then they faded into the night, only to reappear in Dublin. From here they headed for Wales where they surfaced at Cardiff. Fraudulent bills of exchange were turning up everywhere. The West Country was not neglected; Minehead and Barnstaple both suffered from the brothers' visits.

There was, however, a large hiccough at Warwick, where George dallied too long and was arrested. Quickly tried and convicted, he was sentenced to hang. Luckily Joseph was able to grease a few palms, thus helping his brother to escape.

After Warwick, they turned their felonious talents to the smuggling trade. They had learned the finer points from a free-booter at Dover, later buying their own streamlined cutter and running it from Folkestone to the French coast, dealing in brandy and fine lace.

Profits were good but, as usual, the Westons were only a few precarious steps in front of the authorities. The net, once again, was closing in.

They sold the cutter at a profit, and travelled the length of the country to Edinburgh, where they set up in business, this time as respectable linen drapers. They opened premises in the most prestigious part of the town.

Things were going well, but old habits die hard. George was forging bills of exchange to pay off his wholesalers. It was a short-term policy, and the canny Scots were no mugs where finance was concerned. The brothers were literally run out of town and back over the English border. The Westons retrieved what was left of their stock and headed for Bristol, where they sold what they could in the markets there.

Again with money in their pockets, they headed for London. They had been too long from the bright lights. The capital was large enough to provide them with the anonymity they badly needed.

It was on the journey to London on that cold January night that the Weston brothers overtook the *Bristol Mail*. They were surprised to see it so badly protected. It was a spur-of-the-moment decision to hide up further along the road towards Maidenhead, and then to descend upon the unfortunate post-boy. They suspected they would gain little from this particular endeavour, but anything that supplemented their income was worthwhile.

It was decided that George should ride down and rob the drowsing boy while Joseph would stay behind to head off any aid he might be able to summon.

At 3am, just west of Maidenhead, the plan was put into action. George, a scarf hiding the lower part of his face, rode up to the dozing post-boy. He placed a loaded pistol against his face and demanded that he dismount. The boy panicked. Petrified, he began to shake and scream, his shrieking voice piercing the silent Berkshire moorland. George Weston struck the lad hard on the side of the head with his pistol.

The boy's shouting ceased, and he sat there stupefied. George cracked him again and hauled him off the cart. He then grabbed the reins and drove back along the road, leaving the wounded post-boy to stagger to the nearest village.

At four in the morning, in a lonely field at Lot's Farm near Twyford, the brothers were to realise the enormity of their good fortune. There was sack after sack of mail from Bristol and Bath. Their cornucopian haul was to realise more than £10,000 in bills and banknotes, thus making it the largest highway robbery yet to be achieved.

It was the sheer size of the haul that was to make the Weston brothers the most famous and the most wanted of all 18th century robbers. It also brought into the case a famous Bow Street Runner, Jack Clarke.

Clarke had already achieved fame as a law enforcer by tracking down and executing the famous dandy highwayman, Jack Rann. He was now in his prime, short and swarthy, and he had a reputation for never smiling and always getting his man. He had the description of the brothers placed in every London newspaper by the following day. Clarke also employed 'whisperers' in every county; men who kept their ears to the ground and, for a suitable reward, forwarded information.

It was such a 'whisperer' who had informed Jack that men answering the brothers' description had been seen drinking in an alehouse on Winkfield Plain, not five miles from Maidenhead, the day after the robbery. Clarke had arrived there from London. The descriptions were perfect, even to George's crooked thumb, but it was rumoured that they had fled north to Newcastle after spending some time in the Midlands. The brothers had money to burn and they were often in disguise, George specialising in the part of a naval officer, Joseph as his valet.

Jack Clarke knew that sooner or later the brothers would show up in London and, as soon as they did, his network of spies would ferret them out. He was not disappointed. It was Christmas 1781 when news filtered through that they were celebrating at the Red Lion at Bishopsgate (an inn later to be made famous by Dickens's *Old Curiosity Shop*). Clarke surrounded the building, but the brothers had been forewarned and had absconded.

It was not until March in 1782 that the brothers made the error that was the beginning of their undoing.

The Westons were now well-to-do, and there was no necessity for work, either of a lawful or unlawful kind. They had sufficient education and style to carry it off as gentlemen. This they had done when they descended on the genteel town of Winchelsea. They had hired two massive and attractive, expensive houses, and were accompanied by two attractive and expensive lady friends. The air of respectability suited them well.

The good life might well have gone on indefinitely. Clarke's trail was cold, and detection seemed remote. The trouble was that George had a needling propensity for deception that could not be slaked. He had adorned his new abode at Winchelsea with the finest furniture from a firm in London's New Bond Street and, although well able to afford it, he had failed to pay. Hence, after many warnings, the London company had contacted the Sheriff of Rye to collect the debt.

When the Sheriff and his men approached the brothers at Winchelsea, they found them in a state of drunken revelry. George and Joseph, accompanied by their ladies, fired pistols in the air, and were then chased by the Sheriff through the streets of the town. They dispatched their excess female baggage at the Strand Gate where the Sheriff was closing in on them, and then headed across the quicksands to Rye, where they left their horses and disappeared among the labyrinth of smuggler's passageways that honeycombed the cobbled streets.

Unfortunately, one of the Sheriff's impromptu posse had earlier been drinking with the brothers and had noticed George's notorious mutilated thumb. Looking through wanted notices later on, he had picked out George and a reward-seeking Sheriff had got in touch with Jack Clarke.

The Weston brothers headed to Margate and then once again they reached the continent at Antwerp, by way of a diversion, later returning to London *via* the back door at Tilbury. But Clarke had posters and whisperers at all the ports and the moment they returned, the wily Runner knew it.

Clarke had his quarry followed to London. He watched as they settled in a smart hotel in Wardour Street, and then he slowly and stealthily surrounded the place with Bow Street Runners. His moment had arrived, and he intended to savour it.

At seven o'clock in the evening, a time Clarke judged opportune, he and his fellow-officers burst into the brothers' bedroom. The Westons drew pistols, fired into the ceiling and,in the confusion, leapt through an open casement to the ground below. More runners converged on them and a chase ensued. They fled across Wardour Street, down what is now Sheraton Street and Carlisle Street and into Soho Square. Soho Square in the 1780s was a marshalling place for sheep and cattle. It was the brothers' intention to disappear in the ensuing melée. The attempt was doomed to failure as the brothers were vastly outnumbered. Within seconds they had been cornered, overpowered and finally arrested. The sibling miscreants were in the grasp of the relentless and merciless Jack Clarke.

George and Joseph Weston were lodged at Newgate while awaiting trial. The prison had been destroyed by fire previously, and then rebuilt in 1780, only to be badly damaged the same year by the Gordon Riots. At that time nearly 300 prisoners had been released by the mobs. Much of the old building was still in disrepair when the brothers were incarcerated.

On 15 May 1782 the Weston brothers stood trial at the Old Bailey for the Great Mail Robbery, England's most famous and costly crime. The prosecution was in a bit of a quandary; the main witness, the teenage post-boy, had been inconsiderate enough to die on the day the trial began. What were they to do now? The only witness to the robbery had met his demise possibly due to the blows to his head sustained during the robbery. Should the prosecution now try them for the distinguished Great Mail Robbery or for murder?

The prisoners were returned to Newgate while lawyers deliberated.

During this brief lapse in proceedings, the Westons became possessed of pistols and a file. This is possibly not so unbelievable when you remember their affluence and how loudly money talked, nay shouted, in the 1780s. However, the brothers filed through their shackles and made a desperate and final bid for freedom.

It was doomed to failure. They had set upon the turnkey, knocking him unconscious, and then gathering his keys, made for the gate. George got no further, being hauled down by guards and fellow-prisoners. Joseph had made it through the gate, but was cornered by the populace in an alley. He fired and wounded a porter before being retaken. This action was to cost young Joseph his life.

The new trial opened in July 1782. The officials had opted for the more prestigious *Royal Mail* charge, rather than the more tenuous one of murder of the post-boy. The public had been most incensed at the relative simplicity with which the *Royal Mail* company had been relieved of their entrusted money. As both crimes carried an automatic death sentence, along with many others, so far as the prisoners were concerned, any specific charge was purely academic.

As the main witness to England's largest robbery had now passed on, the evidence against the Westons was flimsy indeed. Inevitably the brothers were acquitted, only to be hastily rearrested, George for countless frauds, and Joseph for wounding the porter with intent to kill.

Both were convicted and sentenced to hang, ironically for a mass of mundane crimes, and not for the *Royal Mail* robbery that had made them so famous.

The Weston brothers walked together to Tyburn on 3 September 1782. They asked that their wrists be untied. This, their last wish, was respected, and George and Joseph went to meet their maker hand in hand.

THE WESTON'S ESCAPE ROUTE TAKES THEM TO ANTWERP BY WAY OF MARGATE, HERE IN 1781. (DS)

THE WESTONS SETTLED IN RYE, WHICH LOOKED LIKE THIS IN THEIR DAY. (GB)

ELIZABETH'S EFFIGY — THE HOBY MEMORIAL AT BISHAM CHURCH. (TM)

Bisham's Heartless Lady

Bisham's medieval Abbey stands alongside the river Thames, just a few miles from Marlow. Much of the original building has gone, replaced by fine Tudor brickwork. The old building, seen from the Thames on summer days, is quietly and broodingly majestic.

Let us not dwell on the early inhabitants of the Abbey for that would run to a *Who's Who* of our heritage. It has connections with the Knights Templar, Henry VIII, Anne of Cleves and Queen Elizabeth I.

Our story begins with the death of Henry VIII. He had promised the Abbey buildings to Anne of Cleves, but had not put his Royal seal to the document, leaving Anne in something of a predicament after his death.

When Edward VI succeeded, he order Anne to exchange Bisham Abbey for a less grandiose abode in Kent, owned by his old friend, Philip Hoby. Philip Hoby, a man of considerable wealth, built today's fine Tudor residence. In 1558 the Hoby family became firmly entrenched as Lords and owners of Bisham.

Philip Hoby died there shortly after completing the house and was succeeded by his younger brother, Thomas. Thomas took himself a wife, Elizabeth Cooke, one of the three Cooke sisters, who greatly influenced society in their day. The eldest sister married Sir William Cecil, and was the mother of Robert Cecil, who became Queen Elizabeth's Secretary. The second sister was the mother of Sir Francis Bacon, and the youngest, Elizabeth came to Bisham as Lady Hoby.

Lady Elizabeth Hoby was a striking woman in more ways than one; her portrait seems to endow her with more strength and resolution than actual good looks. She was extremely accomplished in the classics, speaking both Greek and Latin fluently. She had been, in fact, tutor to the young Princess Elizabeth, who was a virtual prisoner at Bisham before succeeding to the throne. Lady Hoby was also a martinet and believed that learning could only be achieved through hard work and discipline.

The record shows that the Hobys had four children — two sons and two daughters. Elizabeth took over their schooling herself and they seem to have inherited her intellect. Their progress is well documented. There was, however, another child, a William Hoby, whose pedigree was a little doubtful and whose very birth would seem to be a little obscure. He is mentioned but seldom in any of the family records that were kept so meticulously. The first four children appear in the archives with regularity, as does Francis, a child born to Elizabeth and Lord John Russel, a man she married some eight years after the death of Thomas Hoby in Paris in 1566.

Who William was, we can only surmise, but he certainly did not have the intellectual capabilities of his brothers and sisters. He was dull, untidy in his books, arrogant and morose, with slovenly characteristics that hardly endeared him to his perfectionist mother. Untidy work led to rows, rows led to confrontation, confrontation led to the boy being soundly thrashed by his exasperated mother.

As to how young William met his untimely death, accounts vary. One school of thought has it that William received his regular thrashing for untidy work and was then locked up in a tiny room to rewrite it. His mother in the mean time was summoned to London (some say Windsor) for an audience with the Queen.

On returning from Court some days later, Lady Elizabeth enquired the whereabouts of her son, William, having completely forgotten locking the child in before she left, and not telling the servants she had done so. The door was hastily opened, but too late to save the life of poor William, who had starved to death.

Another hypothesis, which is really an adaptation of the first, is that Lady Hoby, finding the boy's shoddy work, thrashed him across the head and shoulders with a blackthorn stick and then found out, too late, that she had gone too far — William was dead. She then fled to the Queen in London, feigning surprise on her return.

This would seem the more likely of the two stories. If the first were correct, surely a house full of children and servants would have heard poor William's pleas and, even if they had been too frightened of his mother's retribution to release him, surely they would have passed him food.

William's actual existence is not in doubt; ink-blotted and tear-stained schoolbooks, with the name William Hoby on the cover, were discovered in 1840 by some workmen during reconstruction work. Was William a love child, kept in the background because of the embarrassment, or were most of the records of his existence obliterated after his untimely death, to give solace to a stern and autocratic murderess? We shall never know.

Elizabeth Hoby died at a great age in 1609, after spending her final days painstakingly and efficiently planning her own funeral, down to the minutest detail. Any guilt she many have felt for the loss of her son did not affect her longevity. Her memorial in Bisham Church is one of the finest in the country.

It is possible that she acquired a posthumous conscience for, over the years, there have been many well-attested witnessings of her shade, wringing its hands — at the fate of William?

BISHAM ABBEY THEN AND NOW. (CB)

PHILIP YALE DREW WITH SUPPORTERS OUTSIDE THE CORONER'S COURT.

The Reading Cash-Killing

Ascot and Windsor race meetings in the twenties were a trying time for the respectable county town of Reading. They drew an entourage of unseemly types; successful gamblers in high spirits and unsuccessful ones drowning their sorrows brought discord to the rapport of this suburban bastion of courteous society. The gamblers were often accompanied by street performers, vendors, pickpockets, women of ill-repute and down-and-outs of every degree. Such a day was Saturday, 22 June 1929, Black Saturday to the locals — the day of the influx.

Mr Alfred Oliver sat behind the counter of his tobacconist's at 15 Cross Street, a small connecting street joining the parallel Broad and Friar Streets. He was a contented, if not an ambitious man; he took pride in his shop, which he looked upon as more of a gentlemen's club. Professional men would look in to buy cigars and while away the time, and Alfred Oliver was an expert on cigars and respectful,if not servile, to his auspicious customers.

Imagine the scene: it is close on six on the Saturday evening; it is his intention to close the shop at about six-thirty. Mrs Oliver is walking the dog, Alfred has washed and tidied away the tea things while keeping an eye on the shop from the adjoining neat and spotlessly clean flat. Customers are sparse, as most are at home for their evening meals. He regains his seat behind the mahogany counter, a holiday brochure in hand. He peruses it and, as he and his wife will be starting their annual vacation the following Monday, Teignmouth is decided upon. A customer comes in and half a crown is placed on the counter for cigarettes. As Alfred Oliver begins to rise, a blunt instrument is smashed forcibly upon his head, followed by more blows incessantly raining down upon the elderly tobacconist. Alfred Oliver finally crumbles in a heap behind his polished mahogany counter. His assailant reaches over, pulls the cash drawer from the till, empties it of its £12 in notes and walks into the sunlit Reading streets.

Mrs Oliver returned at 6.15. She came through the front door of the shop and was a little surprised at not seeing her husband behind the counter. She then opened the door to the flat and called out 'Olly'. There was no reply. Perplexed, she turned and noticed the figure of her husband slumped on the floor behind the counter. She rushed to him and cradled his head in her arms.

'What on earth has happened?' she enquired.

'My dear, I do not know.' was Alfred Oliver's brief reply before lapsing once again into unconsciousness.

At this stage his wife did not realise he had been attacked.

Mrs Oliver's first thought was to get help. She dashed across the road to the Welcome Café, owned by her friends, the Taylors. Nellie Taylor was in, but her husband was at Higatt's, the butchers, just a few yards away. George Taylor was collected and he and Mrs Oliver returned to the tobacconists's to be joined shortly by PC Chandler, an off-duty policeman who happened to be in Higatt's too.

Medical help was summoned in the person of the family doctor, Doctor Stanfield. He quickly recognised the severity of Alfred Oliver's wounds and his deteriorating condition. PC Chandler 'phoned his station in Valpy Street, and called for an ambulance to take the wounded man to the Royal Berkshire Hospital.

Initially the case was investigated by a local man, Chief Constable Thomas Burrows but, by Sunday afternoon, Scotland Yard was involved. Two of their most famous and formidable officers were on their way down from Paddington — Chief Inspector James Berret and his inseparable companion, Detective Sergeant John Harris. Of their long list of successes the most recent and most famous was the arrest, conviction and execution of two thugs, Browne and Kennedy, who had heartlessly blasted to death an Essex police constable named Gutteridge.

Berret, as was his sergeant Harris, was a man of immense physical proportions. He stood over six feet and was of an incredible bulk. It was rumoured that he even had his neckties specially made. Both men were as large as their reputations, and each was also well-known for his meticulous and painstakingly thorough methods.

The two CID officers arrived at Reading Station just before 5pm. They were met by two uniformed officers, Pope and Knight, and then whisked off to Valpy Street where Chief Constable Thomas Burrows outlined the case.

There was little to go on. The tobacconist had been viciously attacked, and £12 had been stolen. There was one witness, a Mrs Jackson, who had bumped into a man at the appropriate time, near Oliver's premises in Cross Street, but the good lady was refusing to make a statement without the consent of her husband. Two coats had been stolen from a car at the back of Cross Street, but the thief was later arrested and cleared of the Oliver case. There was little else.

Berret and his companions repaired to the scene of the crime for the inevitable measuring and taking of statements. This done, the Yard's largest, most successful and only bearded detective retired to a tiny room at the Blagrave Arms. There, with a copious supply of scotch, he mulled over the day's events.

His thoughts were interrupted by Sergeant Harris, who had a message from the Royal Berkshire Hospital. Alfred Oliver had died. It was now murder.

On Monday 24 June Berret called in the head of the Yard's fingerprint bureau, Chief Inspector Harry Battley, and a photographic expert, Chief Inspector William McBride. They found little other than a bloodstained impression on a showcase. It was checked against the prints of George Taylor, who had been early on the scene, but they did not match.

Evidence was now beginning to trickle in. Mrs Jackson of Curzon Street reluctantly told Berret of her encounter with a man in Cross Street at the relevant time. She still refused to make a statement, but she would, however, describe the man. He was flurried, middle-aged, but smartly dressed in a blue suit.

Another man to step forward reluctantly was George Charles Jefferies, a 21-year-old messenger boy, who lived in Castle Street with his mother. He, prompted by two friends, blurted out his story.

On Saturday he had been given some time off to visit his critically ill sister, 17-year-old Lillian, as she lay in hospital. That evening, just after six, he had delivered some parcels at the Post Office and then dropped into Oliver's to purchase some cigarettes. Not being able to make anybody hear, he had wandered behind the counter and found Mr Oliver lying there in his grievous state. The condition of his sister still playing on his mind, young Jefferies had fled, saying nothing to anyone until he had read of the seriousness of the crime. He had then reluctantly contacted the police. Asked if it was his half-crown left on the counter, Jefferies said no. He could not afford to leave money behind, however deeply shocked.

After questioning the messenger boy for some three hours, Berret and Harris released him.

Another man who had nothing to do with the murder was an attention seeker, Owen Roberts, a tailor of no fixed abode who admitted the murder when arrested at Pangbourne for another, but trivial offence.

The newspapers had a field day, as the case caught the imagination of the country.

The inquest opened at 2.45pm in a small court in Dukes Street. The coroner was John Lancelot Martin, a personal friend of the deceased, as were several members of the jury.

The first witness was Arthur William Crouch, Oliver's brother-in-law. To him fell the duty of identifying the body.

He was followed by Dr James Leonard Joyce, a specialist at the Royal Berkshire Hospital. Joyce went into a lengthy explanation dealing with how Mr Oliver was admitted on the Saturday evening, and the condition he was in. He stated that, at several times during the following hours, Mr Oliver had been clear-thinking and articulate.

Dr Joyce had enquired what happened, and Mr Oliver had replied that he did not know. The last thing he remembered was reading at his counter. The doctor reported that the patient alternated between the conscious and the disorientated for several hours and then at 5.50 on the Sunday evening, he died.

Dr Joyce conducted a post-mortem on the following Monday 24 June. He discovered thirteen lacerated wounds to the scalp and six wounds to the left ear. There were cuts and abrasions to the lips and jaw and also numerous depressed areas to the base of the skull and a massive fracture across the base of the skull.

Death was due to fractures of the skull and severe cerebral contusion. All the injuries were consistent with an enraged and merciless attack with a blunt instrument.

Speculation came from the jury as to what type of blunt instrument was used; coal hammers, tyre levers and spanners were suggested, even knuckle dusters. Joyce accepted that any one of these weapons may have been used or even two of the same used in conjunction.

Inspector Berret stood up and questioned the doctor: 'Are the injuries consistent with a jemmy or case opener?' he enquired.

'Certainly,' replied Joyce.

What had the inspector in mind? A jemmy might suggest the murderer had gone to burgle the premises. A jemmy is a housebreaker's weapon, not a murderer's. There was little more to be done. Mr Martin adjourned the case *sine die*. He gave his condolences to the widow and said that he hoped whoever had perpetrated this terrible deed would soon be brought to justice.

During the next few days an amazing amount of evidence came to light. Berret and Harris started quizzing local traders, taxi drivers and itinerate travellers.

A Scotsman had been witnessed hammering on the door of the nearby Bull public house. He was described as aggressive; he was also destitute. He was asking local people for money and also approached local clergy. He was later cleared.

A Mrs Dorothy Shepherd described a middle-aged man in a blue suit who had come running from the direction of Alfred Oliver's shop. The man may possibly have been bleeding. A Mrs Loxton saw a similar man.

Mrs Lewington of Wokingham also described a middle-aged man in a blue suit. She said it looked as if he had been fighting.

Mrs Alice James described a man of similar appearance who had rushed past her near Cross Street and she, accompanied by Mrs Lewington and Mrs Loxton, were escorted to Valpy Street to peruse the Criminal Records Office picture gallery.

The newspapers were once more having a heyday. The suspect was described as the 'man in the blue suit', or the 'man with the staring eyes'. They reported, quite correctly, that over a dozen people had witnessed him in or around the vicinity of Cross Street at the appropriate time. Surely an arrest was imminent!

After several days however, with nobody apprehended, the papers indulged in a little poetic licence. Every suspicion became a headline.

Bloodstained clothing was found at Peppard Common, some five miles from Reading, but under analysis the stains turned out to be six months old.

A man in an Isleworth doss house, who was in Reading that day, was suspected, but later released.

A tramp named Frederick Redvers Johns described a man he saw throwing a parcel over a nearby railway bridge on the evening of 22 June. Despite a massive search and assistance from the GWR, the parcel was never traced.

A well-known burglar with a record of violence was arrested in Hyde Park, but no charges were brought.

A young man who booked into a hostelry in London Road, Reading, and refused to give his name, was suspected. He arrived late on 22 June, and disappeared early on the Sunday morning of the 23rd. He was subsequently traced and cleared by Oxford police, who knew him as Stephen Smith, a wandering sheet music salesman.

At the time, the red herrings were too numerous to tabulate, but one man who did receive the most meticulous scrutiny of Inspector Berret, was called Walter Candy.

Candy, a travelling tinker, was arrested on 23 July for attempting to slash a man with a razor. He was remanded for a week. He mentioned to Sergeant Pope that he knew who was responsible for the murder of Oliver. He sounded convincing, and so he was taken before Berret. The story he related was long and imaginative.

Candy, who had a long history of violence, reported that, while he was in Reading on 22 June, an Italian named Mike, whom he knew slightly, approached him and suggested that they rob a shopkeeper in the town. Candy refused and the Italian had wandered off muttering that he would do it alone.

The Italian was soon traced, as his parents had a boarding house in the town. He was also just as quickly cleared, as he could prove his whereabouts all day. The majority of the day he had been at Ascot Races. His evening, including the incriminating hour between six and seven, had been spent in the Oxford Arms, a town pub. There had been several witnesses.

Thus Mike the Italian was cleared, but Berret was still a little unsure of Candy: he fitted well the description of the man in the blue suit. Inspector Berret's suspicions intensified when Alice James and another witness picked him out in a line-up.

Then Candy brought forward a witness who assured police he had been drinking with the prisoner in the Star, another central

Reading public house, at the time of the murder. With nothing further to go on, Berret reluctantly let the wayward tinker go about his business.

Never had Berret come across a case with so many promising openings that led nowhere. He returned to London, leaving Burrows and Harris to run things from Reading.

In Brixton he interviewed yet another man who admitted to the murder but was swiftly cleared. Meanwhile, another suspect was arrested at Southampton. He also was quickly released, but he informed on two other well-known villains, MacDonald and Collins. Both were apprehended but once again there was little to go on. Neither of their photographs was recognised by any of the witnesses. The police had drawn a blank.

Berret sat down dejectedly to write his lengthy report. It was to run to 2,300 pages of foolscap. It seemed impossible that, from such a large and fertile dossier, absolutely nothing had emerged.

On 19 July Sergeant Harris was sitting in Berret's office at the Yard, when the phone rang. It was Inspector Burrows from Reading; 'I think I can establish the identity of the man seen outside Oliver's shop,' he said. Was this the break so badly needed? It was pure chance that Philip Yale Drew came into the frame.

Chief Constable Burrows was outside his club in Friar Street when a fellow-member approached him and suggested he looked into the whereabouts of Philip Drew, an actor who was performing in a play called *The Monster* at Reading's Royal Theatre at the time of the Oliver murder. Burrows, now clutching at straws, looked into it and became more and more interested in the actor. He certainly was in the town on 22 June, and he certainly fitted the description. His photograph had also been vouched for by several of the witnesses. Burrows became more and more convinced that he had the right man.

He traced the theatre company to Nottingham and, joined by Detective Inspector Walters of Reading and Sergeant Harris, awaited the result of enquiries by Nottingham police to see if Drew was still with the company. On 23 July news arrived that he was so, Berret still on holiday, Burrows and Harris went to Nottingham.

They went to Drew's lodging and told him their suspicions. They also persuaded him to sign a declaration stating that he had been cautioned, which enabled them to obtain a set of fingerprints.

They were back in Nottingham again on 29 July, making further enquiries. Drew said that he was an American citizen and would not tolerate such indignities.

The police returned this time to Reading, after obtaining Drew's jacket from a Nottingham dry-cleaners. They found the jacket had been bleached — forensic laboratories could find no trace of blood.

There was no way the police could hold Philip Drew, but this did not stop them following him. They dogged him the length and breadth of the country, wherever the small troupe of players appeared. Under this pressure Drew's disposition alternated to extremes. Sometimes he was confident to the point of arrogance, and sometimes depressed to the point of despair.

Philip Yale Drew was a frightened man. He had been asked to appear at Reading Coroner's Court on 2 October 1929.

Chief Inspector Berret continued to accumulate and tabulate the evidence that he hoped would lead to Drew's indictment.

> He knew that Drew was in Cross Street but Drew denied it.
> He knew Alice James would identify Drew as the man who had seen near Oliver's shop just after six, covered in blood. Drew, on the other hand, could not account for his whereabouts.
> Mr Loxton was sure that it was the actor he had witnessed near the shop at about the incriminating time.

There was also evidence that Drew had visited several other tobacconists, purchasing pipes to send to friends. Philip Drew had also been seen at the relevant time by a stagehand. He was carrying something wrapped in newspaper.

At Maidstone, where the company had moved from Reading, a maid-servant had seen Drew frantically trying to remove a stain from his jacket; the operation had taken half an hour.

Chief Inspector Berret was quietly confident.

Philip Yale Drew was born in a small village near Boston, Massachusetts in March 1880. He was the third of eight children. His parents, although not wealthy, were well-connected. Drew claimed, with more than a little documented substantiation, to be directly descended from Peregrine White, the first white man to be born in America.

As a boy, he was an excellent horseman and also became on good terms with a tribe of Sioux Indians. His first love was the theatre and, as a young man, he plagued local companies for small parts. Finally he was successful. He toured for three years from coast to coast.

In 1904 he met up with a man named Blaney, and Young Buffalo was born. Blaney was writing an extravaganza of the disappearing Wild West and Drew, as Young Buffalo, was to be the star.

Blaney traced many famous old names of the west for his shows and plays. Reality was his byword and Drew's rugged features and dexterity with horses made him a natural choice.

Blaney's success in the States lasted for some years and then, in 1910, the affluent company decided to tour Great Britain.

The King of the Wild West, as the show was now called, took London by storm. The street procession prior to each performance, with real Indians, Mexican bandits and cattle rustlers, enthralled an English public; it brought escapism to their grey walls and drab lifestyles. After London, the show moved to the provinces and appeared at most of the larger towns; the show was to catch the imagination of audiences for a full three years.

After *King of the Wild West* came *The Frozen North*, but that was by no means such a success. Following this came *The Texas Ranger*, to an even worse reception. The company's finances were running low. Drew tried to back the Company with his own resources but, in 1916, a disillusioned set of players returned to the USA.

Philip Drew (Young Buffalo) had a tolerably good run with many films in Hollywood but, finding this unfulfilling, returned to his native Massachussets. Drew never forgot his rapport with the English, and a penchant for their way of life enticed him once again. In 1920 he was back in the West End in a play called *The White Man*.

With alternating success and failure in various new plays Philip Drew once again toured the country. However, things began to take a downward turn in 1923/4 and Young Buffalo was taking to the firewater. His performance was suffering and could be found more and more often in saloon bars, pouring down whisky, and pouring out his life history to some new-found friend. Drew became less punctual, he muffed his lines, and was often replaced by an understudy. Matters went from bad to worse.

Drew left the Company and joined some old friends, Frank and Marion Lindo, in a religious production called *The Rock*. It was a dismal failure.

1926-27 found him hawking a play round London offices with no potential takers. After a succession of small and inadequate parts, fate found Philip Drew with friends Frank and Marion Lindo, performing at the Palace Theatre, Reading, on 17 to 23 June.

The coroner's proceedings were once again opened at Reading Magistrates' Court in Valpy Street, the coroner's court deemed too small for such a case. The date was 2 October, the time 11.25am. The coroner was again Mr John Lancelot Martin.

Mr Martin warned the jury to beware of having their judgement swayed by the unprecedented publicity that had already surrounded the case at local and national levels.

Witnesses were then called, firstly as to the circumstances and the discovery of the body. Among these was young George Jefferies, who explained why he had run out of the shop in fear, and had only contacted the police on the advice of his friends and mother the following day. Jefferies' excuse was accepted and, after a reprimand from John Martin for not behaving like a man, he was asked to sit down.

The most crucial evidence of the day came from Mr Loxton, who worked as a butcher next door to the Oliver's shop. He stated that a man with an accent had been to his shop at about 1.30pm on 22 June. He later went on to say that he had seen the same man in the vicinity about 5.30 to 6.00, and that he seemed to be heading for the Oliver's shop. Loxton was reminded of an earlier statement he had made to the police stating that the time of the second appearance was between 6pm and 6.05pm. Loxton agreed that might well have been the case. Loxton then went on to describe the man: 5′8″-5′9″ tall, clean-shaven, full-featured, wearing a navy blue suit and no hat.

Asked if he recognised anybody in court of that description, Loxton replied, 'Yes sir, that is the gentleman sitting over there.' There was a stunned silence as Loxton pointed to Drew, sitting between his two friends, Frank and Marion Lindo.

Coroner John Martin asked Drew to rise. He also enquired of him if he had any questions for the witnesses.

'No, sir,' was his only reply.

Drew looked shaken when proceedings were adjourned. That day he found it prudent to acquire the services of one Frederick James Ratcliff, a solicitor of Blagrave Street.

The following day, when the court resumed, Mrs Alice James gave evidence. She stated that she was in Cross Street near the Oliver's shop at about 6.10pm. As she looked in the doorway she noticed a man standing there. He was tall, stoutish and dressed in a dark suit. He had no hat, a lot of hair, and was not wearing eye glasses. He was wiping blood from his face and seemed to have been fighting. Mrs James then told the court how she and Mr Loxton had been transported by the police to Nottingham some time later, where she saw the same man in a street there.

The coroner then asked Mrs James if she could recognise the same man in court.

'That is the man there, sir,' she stated, pointing at Drew.

'Are you positive?' enquired John Martin.

'Yes, sir,' replied Alice James with assurance.

Frederick Ratcliffe then subjected Mrs James to a vigorous cross-examination.

Several other witnesses appeared that day, 3 October. Among them was John Ingram, who said that he and others had been drinking with Drew at 1.35pm that lunchtime, and that Drew had mentioned going to Cross Street to get a paper.

John Windle picked out Drew as a man he had seen the worse for drink and in a threatening attitude in Cross Street at 4.20 on 22 June.

Mrs Taylor from the Welcome Café, whose husband had summoned the police at the discovery of Oliver's body, said that between 4.15 and 4.30 on 22 June a man resembling the description given by others had staggered into her café. He had been belligerent and overpowing, and had left about 5.00.

Once again John Martin put the same question, 'Do you recognise that man in this court?'

'That is the man,' replied Mrs Taylor, pointing directly at Drew.

At least another four witnesses placed Drew in or about Cross Street at varying times on the fateful Saturday afternoon. George Nicholson of Eversley described the actor as sliding down a lamppost whilst trying to measure it with his hands. Another man, Herbert Booth, had a drink with him. All seemed to be confident that Philip Yale Drew was their man.

Although it is the coroner's court's function simply to find the cause of death, under what circumstances it happened and who, if anybody, is to be charged and with what, many members of the public plus the national papers were speaking as if Drew had already been indicted.

Drew himself added to the excitement by giving interviews from his luxurious hotel room at the Great Western. Once an actor, always an actor. Evidence at the coroner's court should have given him little confidence in the outcome, but events took an upward turn when Marion Lindo stepped into the witness box.

Marion Lindo claimed that Drew had had lunch with her husband and herself about 2.30 on the Saturday. He had stayed with the couple until 4pm. He was a little the worse for drink and there had been an argument over a bottle of whisky that Drew had in his pocket. Marion had worried that, if he consumed it that afternoon, his performance would suffer that evening. Drew had walked out in a temper. Mrs Lindo followed Drew to his lodgings some ten minutes later. After a confrontation he refused to give her the bottle. A little after five, Drew went out. She once again passed Drew in the street at about 5.10 and then saw him at the theatre at 6.30, when he came into her dressing room to ask if his make-up was correct. 'He did not seem in the slightest upset or nervous.'

Later Miss Francis of Maidstone was to give evidence to the jury. She was the maid at Drew's Maidstone lodgings, who had witnessed the actor spending half an hour in the garden of the premises trying desperately to clean a navy blue jacket. The date was 29 June, one week after the murder.

Much of the visual evidence was contradictory. Many witnesses had placed Drew in Cross Street between 2pm and 5.30pm. Mrs Lindo, however, had sworn that she could account for Drew's movements up to 5pm that evening. Mr Loxton's evidence was shaky as far as time was concerned. The only witness who had identified Philip Drew as the bloodstained man in Cross Street shortly after six was Alice James.

The establishment of time was now of the essence; conflicting evidence came from all quarters. Alfred Fry, stage manager of Drew's company, told the court that he was at the premises in Friar Street when he heard Drew singing at six o'clock; he also saw and spoke to Drew at 6.15.

Drew's landlady, Mrs Mary Goodhall of 9 Kings Meadow, Reading, said that Drew had not gone out that evening until 6.10.

This was confirmed by two neighbours, who witnessed his departure. Another witness reported Drew looking in a butcher's shop window at 6.11. The sightings of Philip Drew that evening had been numerous and well-attested.

The final witness of the day was Detective Constable Charles Woodward. It had been his responsibility to take all the different times and sightings of Drew, and rationalise them. He had paced all the possible routes and timings and, given a small margin of error, had come to the conclusion that Drew could have left his lodging at the witnessed time and appear at the theatre at the attested time seven minutes later. It would just have been possible to detour and commit the murder in Cross Street, but it would have been a very tight schedule indeed.

The inquest was adjourned until Monday 7 October.

Drew returned to the Great Western Hotel, surrounded by crowds of onlookers and journalists. His lawyer, Mr Ratcliffe, advised him to obtain the services of William Fearnley Whittingshall, a brilliant young barrister.

The normally tranquil town of Reading had caught murder fever. Philip Yale Drew was escorted between the Great Western Hotel and the courthouse by a throng of wellwishers. He seemed to be enjoying the notoriety, playing his greatest part, and his press interviews were getting more prolific and more extensive.

On Monday 7 October the police put forward their case. Police Sergeant Herbert Thorpe said that Drew had walked into the station and reported that trousers he had lost earlier had shown up and that he wanted the sergeant to inspect them. They were produced in court, where Sergeant Thorpe explained they had new pockets. The underlying inference was that Drew had had the pockets renewed because of some tell-tale stain.

Then Sergeant John Harris took the stand. He gave evidence as to how he and other officers had approached Drew on 22 July and taken a statement. He had questioned him on his knowledge of Reading, and his whereabouts on 22 June. His question and answer statement, read as evidence, was a series of accusations from Harris, and denials by Drew.

Harris then told the court that he had again approached Drew the following day. This time he had informed him of two witnesses that he had brought to Nottingham, who had subsequently identified him as the man they had seen in Cross Street at the time of the murder.

At this Drew became disturbed and emotional, and said that, if the three people that he had previously named — the Lindos and Norman Stubbs, the stage manager — could not testify that he was at the theatre at the time of the murder, he knew of no-one else who could, but he certainly did not commit any murder, nor was he seen in Cross Street with blood on his face.

When the court resumed at 2.30, Mr John Lawrence, who had acted as stage manager at Reading, gave some inconsequential evidence which inferred that Drew was a violent man and also that a gun had gone missing from the stage props. Coroner Martin shot holes in the evidence and Lawrence was ordered to sit down.

The last evidence of the day came from a man called Povey, a coalman, who said that between 5.05 and 5.25, he had seen a man who he identified as Drew, drunk as a sack in Broad Street (adjacent to Cross Street). He, Drew, was stroking a car as if it were a cat or dog. This brought the first laughs in court and it ended the day's proceedings.

There had in fact been nearly sixty witnesses, all giving varying times of sightings of Drew or somebody very much like him.

The fifth coroner's session opened on Tuesday 29 October. Various witnesses, including shoppers and tramdrivers, gave varying accounts of witnessing Drew or somebody like him at the appropriate time of the murder.

More testimony was given by Sergeant Harris as to the clothing Drew had worn that day. Drew had gone with the Company to Maidstone and Harris gave evidence about the cleaning of his clothing in that town. Drew had denied that the clothing had been cleaned there and insisted that he had sent it to the cleaners in Swansea and Rochdale previously on the tour. Later Harris clashed with the abrasive Fearnley Whittingstall as to whether the actor's hair had been dyed or not.

Harris finished and the packed courtroom sat in pregnant silence waiting for Philip Drew to take the stand, remembering that it was his prerogative whether he did so or not. He had been formally accused of nothing.

After a short adjournment, Fearnley Whittingstall advised the court that his client wished to give evidence. It was to be one of the actor's greatest roles.

Drew acquitted himself well as a witness. He was questioned on his drinking habits, to which he replied that he drank regularly and too much, but never to the stage where it affected his memory or his thespian ability.

He was then questioned about his arrival time at the theatre and also on his route there from his lodgings. He was vague about both, but vehemently denied travelling *via* Cross Street.

After Drew answered questions concisely on the time taken for the application and removal of make-up, a rather over-zealous coroner once more closed the proceedings.

On Wednesday 9 October proceedings resumed, this time at Reading's small Town Hall. Queues for the public seats had begun at 4am. At 11.50 Philip Drew pushed his way through the massive crowd of onlookers. At 12 noon Mr Martin opened court.

Drew once again took the stand, and he was once again questioned about his movements on 22 June. He was reminded of the statements of the stableman who had joined him for a drink at the Bull, situated at the end of Cross Street, and of the café owner where he had stopped for a fried breakfast. Drew admitted that they might well be correct as he could not remember. Drew was again noncommittal about his movements on the Saturday evening.

Martin then asked Drew about the trousers which had mysteriously, if not conveniently, disappeared in Reading, to show up later on the tour. Once again Drew had no explanation.

Drew was also questioned about his late return to his lodgings that night. His landlady had said that Drew had returned in a dishevelled state about 1.00am from the opposite direction from the theatre.

Mr Lindo was next to take the oath. He and his wife were Drew's best friends and fellow performers. Frank Lindo was a hostile witness from the start. He gave evidence of Philip Drew's character and also stated that on 22 June he had been to the cinema in the afternoon. He had left at 5.30 and heard Philip Drew's voice as he arrived at the theatre at 6.00.

Mr Martin immediately took him to task, reminding him that,in an earlier statement to the police, he had informed them that he had not left the cinema until six. Frank Lindo replied that he could have left the cinema later than 5.30, but he had definitely heard Drew in the theatre at 6.00.

It was now time for the surprise witness, and the one who, without a doubt, had the most affect on the outcome. Fearnley Whittingstall called Alfred John Wells.

Had it not been for the adroitness and presence of mind of two reporters for the *Empire News* and *Daily News* respectively, Alfred Wells, butcher's assistant, would probably never have taken the stand at Reading's most famous coroner's inquest. The young reporters had spoken to Wells soon after the murder. Wells, who worked for Geary's at 22 Cross Street, almost opposite Oliver's tobacconist, had described a man in the near vicinity whose description did not completely tie in with many of the other witnesses.

O'Donnell, the reporter, had realised that Wells was not on the list of witnesses and wondered why. He knew that Wells had gone to the police and, in a public-spirited way, had volunteered a written statement that was taken down by the acting Sergeant, yet a statement which the police had not presented. Spurred by a sense of a possible injustice, O'Donnell, with his journalist colleague, told Fearnley Whittingstall.

Alfred Wells described a man of 5′9″-5′10″ tall, middle aged, with long hair, a north country accent, and wearing a navy blue jacket, grey trousers and brown shoes. (This was much the general description of Drew.)

Wells had first noticed the man when he was breakfasting in the Welcome Café in Cross Street at 7.30am. The man had entered and asked for the lavatory. He had noticed the same man several times during the day, culminating about 5.40pm when he noticed him on the corner of Cross Street and Friar Street.

Fearnley Whittingstall asked the young butcher if he would recognise the man again.

'Certainly,' he replied.

'Would you stand up please, Mr Drew?' requested the barrister.

Philip Drew complied.

'Is this the man?' he asked Wells.

'Certainly not,' replied the butcher. The court was stunned.

'I told the police in my statement that the man's hair was long and dishevelled. It would be impossible with such crinkly hair as Mr Drew possesses.'

Drew sat down.

The coroner spoke sharply to Wells, asking him about his statement and why he had not followed it up. Wells replied that he was a busy man and that by going to the police he considered that he had discharged his public duty.

Wells was requested to take the oath on whether he had actually made a statement, as the police seemed to have no record of it. He insisted that he had and that the officer to whom he had dictated it was on duty controlling crowds outside the courtroom door.

The officer was duly fetched in and asked whether or not he had taken a statement from Wells. Sergeant Arthur Colbert said he could not remember doing so.

Chief Constable Burrows was then called to see if he could throw any light on the missing statement. Burrows stated that they had taken some seventy statements that night and he could not remember the Wells document.

At this point the coroner received a sheet of paper from the table where a host of detectives sat. The missing statement was handed over.

Read out aloud, it seemed to bear out word for word what Alfred Wells had recalled on oath in court.

'This would seem to clear matters up,' said the coroner; 'we will adjourn until tomorrow when I will sum up.'

Once again Philip Yale Drew left for the Great Western Hotel surrounded by wellwishers and admirers. It had been his day and his entourage were glowing with potential satisfaction. Members of the opposite sex, from adolescents to grannies, blew him kisses and wished him 'Good luck'.

On Thursday 10 October the crowd outside the small Town Hall was massive. Drew blew kisses to his supporters and shouted 'God bless you all' as he mounted the steps.

As the proceedings opened there was an immediate head to head confrontation between Fearnley Whittingstall and Mr Martin, the coroner. Fearnley Whittingstall wished to address the jury, but the coroner refused him the right to do so.

John Martin's summing-up took some time. He warned the jury that they were not there to judge anybody, but to decide how the unfortunate Mr Oliver had died, and if there was sufficient evidence to bring criminal proceedings against anybody. He mentioned the unusual event of Drew losing his trousers on Sunday 23rd, to turn up mysteriously at St Albans later on the tour. He mentioned the unshakeable evidence of Alice James and William Loxton, both of whom had identified Drew, both at Reading and Nottingham, also of Mrs Shepherd of Cross Street and her condemning evidence. He at length quoted the evidence given by Wells, the butcher and pointed out that, if the jury believed this and the evidence of Drew's landlady, Mrs Goodall, then it was in direct contradiction to the majority of other witnesses. Finally the coroner sat down.

It was exactly 11.35am when the jurors filed out.

After 2¾ hours of nailbiting frustration the foreman led the way back in. The roll of eleven names was called out by the coroner's officer. Then there was silence.

Mr Martin stood and asked if they had reached a verdict.

'We have, sir,' he replied.

'Please read it,' asked the coroner.

'Mr Coroner, the jury have, after very careful deliberation on all the evidence submitted to them, unanimously agreed that the evidence is too conflicting for them to definitely establish the guilt of any particular person, consequently they return a verdict of wilful murder by a person or persons unknown.'

Drew turned to Mrs Lindo and mouthed 'Thank God'. The court erupted into a crescendo of cheers and applause, and a succession of ever-increasing acclaimation as the news was greeted by the multitude outside.

When order was briefly restored, the coroner thanked the jury and closed the inquest on Alfred Oliver.

Only those who have experienced mass hysteria close at hand can have the slightest concept of Philip Drew's triumphant return to the Great Western Hotel for the last time. Women wept with emotion and relief, flowers were thrown, cheering men were everywhere. Stalwart police by the dozen shouldered a narrow gangway through the human forest.

Wellwishers had blocked the short journey from the court to the hotel. A frenzied throng of waving people barred the attempts of Drew, on the shoulders of four of his largest supporters, to advance.

At length he reached his hotel and was thrust through the front doors by the sheer momentum of the crowd. The doors were then blocked by a dozen or more police.

As Philip Drew approached the balcony window for his most appreciated role before his largest audience, hotel maids and Latin waiters wept uncontrollably. From the balcony he thanked his many friends for their support, and the Lord God for showing the jury his divine wisdom.

It was Drew's finest hour. He took encore after encore until the thinning crowd finally disappeared into the dark autumn evening.

Nobody was ever officially convicted for the murder of Alfred Oliver. The police kept up their enquiries and one or two likely candidates rose to the surface, but nothing was clearly actionable. A man was actually charged with the crime at a Glasgow police station after walking in out of the blue and making a confession. The charges were dropped when his family proved that he was nowhere near Reading on 22 June.

The murder of Alfred Oliver remains a mystery.

But what of Philip Drew? His acting career went slowly but definitely downhill. After a torrid love affair, he lived in abject poverty, telling his story to anyone who would listen for the price of a drink. He blamed his downfall on the 'Reading affair'. He had been found guilty by inferred accusation, and this had ruined his career. Apparently there is such a thing as bad publicity.

Drew died of cancer of the larynx at Lambeth Hospital in 1940, aged 60. He was laid to rest in Chingford Cemetery in a public grave.

LEFT: THE FORMIDABLE DETECTIVE INSPECTOR BERRET AND
RIGHT: MR ALFRED OLIVER, THE MURDERED NEWSAGENT.

BROAD STREET, READING IN THE '20s (CB)

THE SCENE OF THE CRIME — THE COTTAGE AT SALT HILL, SLOUGH.

QUAKER SLAIN AT SLOUGH

John Tawell was not a native of Slough; he was born in the Norfolk village of Aledby, some 200 years ago in 1784.

Nothing is known of him until, at the age of fourteen, he took up a sort of apprenticeship with a widow near Lowestoft. The widow, a Quaker, would seem to have been a devotee of herbal medicine and various other quack cures. Tawell would hack these commodities the length and breadth of East Anglia, his articulate speech and winsome ways expanding the business and reaching some of the hierarchy of that rural society.

For several years the business went from strength to strength. Young John became more and more acceptable and developed strong ties with the aristocracy and the business world. Tawell was a charmer, an opportunist, a socialite and a womaniser, but on the surface he remained respectable. To endorse this he was writing to a young Quaker girl in Norwich with the intention of marriage.

At twenty John Tawell made an important friend in Walter Hunton, a wealthy linen draper from London. Hunton (unfortunately later to be hanged for highway robbery) took Tawell into his firm and virtually set the young man up.

That same year John unfortunately impregnated an Ipswich barmaid, who insisted on marriage, and he complied.

On the death of Hunton, John was out of a job, but he had learned much. He returned to the medicine trade and peddled his goods throughout London and the eastern counties. His living was opulent, colourful and apparently even honest. The drawback was his rather dowdy wife and their increasing brood of children, an imposition to be endured.

John did not fall foul of the law for some ten years until, 1814, when he was accused of forging a £2,000 bond from a bank in Uxbridge. As the penalty for this was death, and as John had affected the ways and dress of a Quaker, the bank manager, a Quaker himself, was somewhat loathe to bring charges.

The police were adamant that a charge should be made. The bank manager was just as adamant that he would not send this respectable young man to the gallows. The result was the great British compromise; Tawell would be charged with the lesser crime of possessing a forged bond rather than actually forging it. For that Tawell was transported to Australia indefinitely.

In Sydney things went well from the start. His intelligence marked him out from other prisoners. It was not long before his medical knowledge had ingratiated him with the prison doctor and afforded him all sorts of privileges. After four years John was released.

As a free man in a growing country, it did not take him long to see the potential. After a few months he had borrowed enough money to set up a drug store in Sydney. After two years he had half-a-dozen going concerns all around the city. Some five years later his establishments had trebled and he was once again the wealthy socialite. His rising affluence and position in society was meteoric and considerable.

The one drawback was that news of his success had travelled back to England. His infuriated wife, who had learned little of him since his departure, and had in all probability imagined him on a chain gang in some inhospitable region, had since learned that her husband was enjoying a rich existence with the high rollers of Sydney. With strong support from her friends she had managed to raise sufficient finances to enable her and her family to travel to Australia.

On arrival in the New World, Tawell's wife found that her husband had amassed an immense fortune. He had also amassed a prolific following of female devotees, several of whom were anticipating betrothal and all of whom were surprised to hear of her existence. John once again had his wings clipped. He decided to return home and become the wealthy and considerate family man.

Tawell's life in England, if domesticated, was never dull. He installed his wife and family in a large London house, and for three years plied a profitable export trade between England and Australia. This necessitated several long sea-crossings. It was on one such that Tawell lost his eldest son, now a man in his mid-twenties. This would seem to be one of the few events that had any lasting emotional effect on him. He was for some time a broken man.

In 1835 Tawell's wife suffered ill-health. She had been a somewhat delicate woman for some years and the long and perilous sea voyage to Australia had taken its toll.

Tawell had engaged a nurse, one Sara Hart, a pretty and efficient young lady, who came highly recommended. Apparently it did not take her long to provide services for both husband and wife. She inevitably became pregnant and conveniently, Mrs Tawell died.

In what sequence these events took place, history does not say. It does relate, however, that Tawell retained Sara Hart's services after his wife's death and rewarded the young lady with a second child. They were blissfully happy for the next two or three years.

Then in 1838, Tawell became infatuated with a widow, a Mrs Cutforth, a headmistress at Berkhampstead School in Hertfordshire.

Once again the lady involved was a Quaker. For some obscure reason, Tawell was convinced that installing himself in the company of such a simple and pious set would give him a veneer of respectability, however he conducted himself otherwise.

This time the Quakers were not going to wear it. Mrs Cutforth had been the wife of one of their most devout followers and they were not going to approve a marriage to this worldlywise womaniser and scoundrel, however financially well endowed he might be.

Mrs Cutforth became the second Mrs Tawell regardless of their feelings. Whereas they made it clear to his wife that they would never forsake her, they also made it clear to Tawell that he would never be accepted. Nonetheless, the Tawells moved into a house at Berkhampstead with the widow's teenage daughter.

Tawell now found Sara Hart a nagging inconvenience, and so he shifted her nd the children to a cottage at Salt Hill near Slough. In those days it was a picturesque village a couple of miles from the pleasant and compact town.

Although his new wife knew of his past, including the part played by Sara Hart and her two young offspring, Tawell could not ignore them and decided to do something about it.

It is always a surprise why people like Tawell resort to the ultimate solution, when there are other courses open to them. There are hundreds of cases of men who took the most drastic and precarious actions to rid themselves of, what is after all, a minor irritant.

Why John Tawell took such action we shall never know. Sara Hart was not his wife, was no longer his mistress, and could not have affected him financially. The pittance that he allowed her to keep herself and his two children could not make much of a dent in Tawell'smore than robust bank account.

Yet he collected two phials of prussic acid from Bishopsgate and proceeded to Sara's cottage at Salt Hill, arriving slightly after 4pm on 1 January. He played with his children and then suggested that she go to the nearby Windmill Inn for some beer, as travelling had parched his throat. Sara detected something unusual in Tawell's attitude. She mentioned this to the barmaid while obtaining the beer.

What happened next is a matter of supposition, terminating with John Tawell racing swiftly away from the scene and Sara screaming and moaning from the cottage. Mary Ashley, Sara's neighbour, saw the rapidly disappearing figure, and asked him what was amiss. Tawell ignored the inquiry and hurried on.

Mary Ashley discovered Sara in severe discomfort and pain. A local doctor was quickly on the scene, but Sara Hart was already dead. The doctor, a man named Champney, realised he could do no more for her but, on hearing of the stranger (Mary Ashley did not know Tawell, but described him as a Quaker), he set out to trace him.

Tawell had reached Slough station, but boarded a coach that ran west towards Windsor. Then he got off and set off back towards Slough. This was unusual behaviour which, unfortunately for him, was noted by the driver. Obviously this was a ruse to throw would-be pursuers off the scent. He walked back into Slough and caught the 7.45 to London.

Tawell's second piece of bad luck was when the tenacious Dr Champney, who had been searching the countryside for the dark-robed perpetrator of the crime, noticed him boarding the train. The resourceful doctor immediately asked the railway staff to use the new electric telegraph to contact the police at Bishops Road terminus.

A Sergeant Williams in London followed Tawell from the train around several of the capital's coffee houses before he returned to Quaker's lodgings at Cheapside. Williams, certain that he had not been detected by Tawell, returned to his office, confident that Tawell had retired for the night.

The police raided at 7am, but Tawell had already absconded; he was later arrested at the Jerusalem coffee house, known to be a favourite haunt.

Tawell, who was deeply affronted that such a respectable businessman should be arrested on such a charge, exclaimed that he had never heard of Sara Hart, nor of Salt Hill, and he had definitely never been there. Despite such protests, he was formally arrested and taken to Eton Police Station. He was charged with the murder of Sara Hart and then escorted to Aylesbury Prison to await trial.

Tawell's official trial began on 17 March 1845. The newspapers had been trying him ever since his arrest. He had already been dubbed the 'Quaker murderer'. It started at 9am, before Judge Baron Parke, and the first day's proceedings did not finish until 11pm. During the trial, over thirty prosecution witnesses were called. They included railway and police personnel, Mary Ashley, a coach driver, the chemist from whom Tawell had purchased the prussic acid, and the barmaid of the Windmill Inn. All the evidence was damning, but none more so than the cool, deliberate and detailed account of Dr Champney.

The public was incensed against Tawell and emotions ran high, inflamed by the melodrama of Sara's mothers, fainting theatrically while giving evidence.

Tawell's alibi was simply disbelieved. It had been too speedily initiated for he had not had time to construct anything at all plausible. Much of his defence consisted of friends giving evidence as to his quality of character.

Tawell did, however, try on a version of the events he hoped would be believed. He said he had visited Sara Hart on 1 January as a New Year's greeting. She had gone out to the Windmill for ale while he contented himself in the kitchen. When Sara returned they drank the ale and she brought up the subject of an increased allowance for her and the children.

Tawell replied that he was short of money, a fact that was later found to be true. Riotous living had drained his fortune. Sara would not believe him, and a row ensued. She had already been in her cups, and became hysterical, and then suicidal. Before he could stop her, she had poured the contents of a small phial into her ale, consumed it, and almost immediately fallen to the floor. Tawell had panicked and fled.

This account of events certainly fitted the circumstantial evidence, but was seen by the jury as most improbable.

Tawell's counsel, Fitzroy Kelly, had already insulted the jury's intelligence by suggesting that prussic acid found in Sara's body was due to eating too many apples. Little was known about the substance in those days, but this form of defence, relying mainly on the naivety of the jury, was met with the derision it deserved. Commonsence told them that anyone could eat dozens of apples a day without suffering any permanent ill effect.

The trial went into its third day, mainly for the judge's summing up. This lasted for four hours, from eight in the morning until a little after noon. The jury were less deliberative; they returned a unanimous verdict of guilty.

Tawell was visibly shaken. He had taken it for granted that his verbose and glib explanation of the facts would convince the jury of his innocence. He had even been confident enough to order a celebration dinner at the White Hart Hotel in Aylesbury for that evening.

As Judge Baron Parke passed the death sentence, John Tawell knew there was no hope. The appeal system was non-existent in 1845.

He died on the scaffold in Aylesbury market square on 28 March 1845, after confessing to the murder while in prison.

Much of John Tawell's adventurous and notorious life has been forgotten, but he does remain exclusive in criminal history, as the first man to be trapped by electric telegraph.

TAWELL IN COURT AT AYLESBURY. (CB)

THE JURY IN THE SLOUGH KILLING CASE. (CB)

EXECUTION

OF JOHN TAWELL,

D FULL CONFESSION, TO HIS WIFE, IN A LETTER

Of the Murder of Sarah Hart.

Aylesbury,
This morning, 8 o'clock.
early hour this morning, fs, with their usual at- arrived at the prison, and aking of some refresh- eeded to the condemn- here they found the re- linary engaged in prayer wretched culprit.
he usual formalities had erved of demanding the f the body of the prison- eir custody, Tawell was l to the press-room, s irons were struck off. utioner, with his assist- commenced pinioning which operation they nd quickly despatched. ese awful preparations deeply, but uttered not At a quarter before 8, rangements having been l, the bell of the prison ed tolling, and the me- procession was formed:— nd ordinary, preceding t on his way to the fatal an reading in a distinct

sort of scream, and saw the prisoner coming out of Mrs. Hart's house. I said, I am afraid my neighbour is ill; but the prisoner, who appeared agitated, made no reply. When I got inside her door, deceased was lying on the floor, with her petti-

chemist, and was formerly lecturer on chemical jurisprudence. Mr. Champneys and two other gentlemen called on me and requested me to test the contents of a human stomach, which they produced in a bottle, another bottle with some

ill, and vomitted about a hand. bason full. Deceased laid the blame on the stout.

The jury returned a verdict of guilty, and the judge pronounced sentence of death upon him.

Copy of a Letter from the Pri-

actions. After living 15 years in Sydney, he returned home, where he has been endeavouring to gain admittance as a member of the Society of Friends, to which body he belonged before his transportation, but they would not admit him. During his first wife's illness, the deceased nursed her, whence arose their illicit correspondence.

COPY OF VERSES.

GOOD people all of each degree
Attend to what I shall unfold.
It is a dreadful tragedy
Will make your very blood run cold.
Your hearts alas with grief will bleed.
When you this cruel tale shall hear;
There's not been done so vile a deed
Since the days of Courvoisier.

John Tawell is my name 'tis true,
In wealth and splendour once I've dwelt.
A hypocrite I've always been,
Nor meek ey'd mercy never felt.
My first crime was Forgery,
A convict was to Sidney sent.
I riches gain'd oh! misery,
My stubborn heart did not relent.

To lustful passions I gave way,

TAWELL TAKES THE DROP.

LITTLECOTE HOUSE.

LITTLECOTE'S BURNING BABE

The Tudor facade of Littlecote is, to say the least, architecturely attractive, but possible a little austere on a misty morning. It was built in 1490 and for much of the time it was owned by the Darrel family. The last and most notorious of this respectable lineage was Wild William Darrel.

Our story really begins in 1575, on a wet and blustery night in the tiny hamlet of Shefford Woodlands. Two riders approached the small cottage of Mrs Barnes, the local midwife. They knocked, gained entrance and offered the lady a large amount of money if she would abide by certain conditions and would never breathe a word of anything that happened on that fateful night.

The startled midwife was blindfolded and placed on the back of one of the horses and taken through the stormy night to a large house. She knew there was something untoward afoot, so she apparently had the presence of mind to count the doors that opened, the strides she took and the stairs she mounted. Finally she was ushered into a large and expensively furnished bedroom. Once in, the blindfold was removed and she noticed two strange occupants. One was a tall, large-featured and forbidding man, dressed in black velvet, and the other was a masked lady, obviously in the last stages of bearing a child.

Mrs Barnes set to work immediately and, a few minutes later, the child was born. As she turned to greet the father with his offspring, the midwife could not believe her ears: 'Place it on the fire,' he commanded. Horrorstruck, she refused. 'Place the brat on the fire,' he thundered. Again she refused. At this point Darrel snatched the child from her arms, strode to the open fireplace, pressed it against the blazing logs with his riding boot and held it there until no more sound came from its tiny body.

It is said that the masked lady died there in childbirth. Other accounts have her dying a week or more later.

While Wild Will Darrel summoned his servants to reward Mrs Barnes and return her blindfolded to Shefford Woods, she seized the opportunity to cut a small piece of material from the drapes in the room. This act was almost the downfall of Will Darrel.

Mrs Barnes, returned to her cottage, amazingly kept her silence for twelve years, only revealing what she knew to a local magistrate,

Anthony Bridges in 1587. It is because of the meticulously kept notes of Mr Bridges that much of this story comes to light at all. Why did the old woman wait so long? Could it be that she had retraced her steps, worked out that the house was Littlecote and the perpetrator of this heinous crime was Darrel? Did she find the first reward insufficient and return again and again for more bites at this financially rewarding cherry? If she did, it was an existence fraught with danger, for she knew very well Wild Will was capable of murder. This would certainly explain why the midwife finally decided to speak when she knew she was close to death.

There was much speculation as to the unfortunate lady in the mask. There are three main contenders.

The first was a Miss Bonham, the sister of a servant of Sir John Thynne. Sir John was a local landowner who had no love for Darrel at all. There had been a war of attrition between the two since Darrel had composed a satire, ridiculing Sir John's mock-Italian attempts at his beloved Longleat, the then home of the Thynnes.

There must have been rumours of the dastardly deed at the hall as early as 1578, for it was in that year that Sir Henry Knyvett (another of Darrel's antagonists) wrote a letter to Sir John at Longleat, asking him to search out Mr Bonham and to enquire how many children his sister had and what had become of them. Obviously Sir Henry Knyvett was suspicious.

Yet the evidence from so many accounts is completely contradictory. If indeed the lady in the mask died at the birth of her child in 1575, what on earth was the good of examining various ladies in 1578?

Let us suppose that the lady did not die, but was whisked into obscurity. This would more easily fit the majority of the accounts, and would also suit the case of the second contender, Caroline Knyvett, wife of the letter writer Sir Henry.

There had been some sort of clandestine liaison between the lady and Darrel for some time. They were often seen together in the extensive grounds of Littlecote and also in the lonely alehouses in the sparse villages of the district. You may well imagine how this type of rumour enhanced Will Darrel in Sir Henry's eyes.

However, the third main contender for the lady of the mask, and the most likely, is Darrel's sister Ada, for several reasons. Firstly, it seems to have been well established at the time that Darrel was having some sort of incestuous relationship with his sister, a woman several years younger but only slightly less wayward than her brother. Secondly, incest was not a rare thing in those days, though as much frowned upon as it is today. What would have caused far more concern to Wild Will would be the existence of a possibly retarded bastard in his home, at his expense.

Another reason for suspecting the masked lady was Ada is that she did seem to disappear, from at least public view, about that time. This would fit the many reports that had the young mother dying in childbirth, for had it been one of the aforementioned ladies Wild Will might well have been rather proud of himself. Illegitimate children were by no means unusual in those days and Darrel would have been rather pleased with the embarrassment caused either of his old antagonists.

Rumour was rife in 1588 and this was the time, armed with the deathbed testimony of Mrs Barnes, and the cutting taken from the drapes of Littlecote (incidentally, the cutting was found to fit the curtains which were sold many years later as a memento to an American), that the lawyers, probably headed by Anthony Brooks, tried to charge Darrel in court.

Here again, reports vary. Some say Darrel was tried and acquitted, others that he was granted a *nolle prosequi* through lack of evidence. Whichever account is true, one thing is sure, and that is that he was never convicted.

Another character turns up at this stage in the obese and blustering form of Judge Sir John Popham. Darrel had mysteriously signed Littlecote over to Sir John in 1586 on the understanding that he would still be allowed to remain. Was this a massive bribe to save Will from a charge of infanticide and possibly the gallows? Probably so, for Darrel was already deeply in debt. Popham probably bought the debts and took Littlecote. There is a school of thought that claims Wild Will was close to coming to court in 1588, four years before Popham became a judge in 1592. In 1588, Sir John Popham was Attorney General and could have brought great influence to bear.

Sir John and his beautiful wife, Mrs Leybourne Popham, enjoyed the ownership of Littlecote for many years and their descendants for generations afterwards. A portrait of a fat and overpowering Sir John is still at the house today and, even allowing for the artist's flattery of his patron, this is a face you would not trust.

But what of Wild Will Darrel? It seems that he was content to stay as a house guest of Sir John Popham for quite a while, though it has been suggested he was thrown into a debtor's prison shortly after the event. If so he cannot have been there long, for in 1589 he was killed under somewhat suspicious circumstances. At Shefford Woodlands, near the border of the Littlecote estate, stood a stile. Even now the area is known as Darrel's stile. In 1589 Wild Will was out riding and was just about to jump the stile on the ancient trackway when it is said the image of a burning baby appeared. The horse shied, throwing Darrel from his saddle; he smashed his head on a nearby stone. Wild Will was dead.

If you drive along the A338 at night and come to the hamlet of Shefford Woodlands, look for a wide track that once was a Roman road, that crosses the main road at right angles, near the picturesquely thatched pub, the Pheasant. You may see the spectre of Wild Will Darrel on a black horse, followed by a couple of hounds, but be careful at the sight of a burning baby. The horse could shy and there could be a fatal accident.

MRS AMELIA DYER, READING'S BABY FARMER

THE READING BABY FARMER

In the town of Cheltenham in January 1896, there was born to an unmarried mother, a daughter named Doris Marmon. The mother was a pretty blonde barmaid called Evalina. Times were hard, and society did not take the same enlightened view of illegitimate children that it does today. Evalina was financially desperate, could not work and also tend the child.

She scanned the newspapers for offers of adoption, of which there were many. One that was more attractively worded than the rest caught her eye. She answered it, and a day or two later, received a reply bearing the postmark 'Caversham'. The writer professed to be church-going, happily married, to have a large house and be infatuated with young children.

The letter seemed to be the answer to her prayers. She just hoped that the lady would not charge too much for taking the child off her hands.

An appointment was made and, when the lady arrived, Evalina was surprised to find someone 60 years old, and of incredible bulk, some 15 or 16 stones, but she seemed sincere. She introduced herself as Mrs Stanfield and appeared genuine. When she said that she only wanted £10 for looking after little Doris, and that her mother could come and visit as often as she liked, a deal was struck and a tearful Evalina waved goodbye to Mrs Stanfield and her small daughter.

Ever since the summer of the previous year, many horrifying discoveries had been made in the Thames near London. These were babies' bodies, over forty of them in various stages of decomposition. None had been stillborn, all had been strangled and the police had decided that one person was responsible for all the murders and that person was a woman.

Less than a month after Mrs Stanfield had returned to Caversham, the God-fearing people of Reading were shocked to find that similar gruesome discoveries were appearing on their stretch of the river. Each child had been strangled with red tape, the other end of which was attached to a brick, that was used to prevent the tiny body rising to the surface.

There were six small bodies in all, three in the Thames near King's Meadow, another in the Kennet, and a further two that the police found when they dragged a local pond called Clapper's Pool.

The first body, found in the Thames, was discovered accidentally by a bargee, who had been poling his way up the river and had been more than mildly surprised when he had brought his pole up from the river bed to find a sodden brown parcel on the end with a baby's arm sticking out. Little did the bargeman know that he would be instrumental in bringing to justice the most hated woman of her time.

This particular parcel bore, on the third sheet, the one closest the body, the smudged but still discernible name and address of a woman in Reading; a Mrs Dyer of Kensington Road.

Detective Inspector Anderson, who was in charge of the case, rushed his men to the house only to find the bird had flown, luckily for him only as far as Caversham. He thoroughly searched the house and came up with some startling and damning evidence. The cupboards were stacked with discarded baby clothing, receipts for adverts in London and suburban newspapers, anxious letters and telegrams from worried mothers, in fact virtually everything to give the thankful Detective Inspector a watertight case.

It did not take long for the police to trace Mrs Dyer to Caversham where she was arrested. In that house there was even more conclusive evidence by the way of pawn tickets, and more letters written to Mrs Stanfield and Mrs Harding, both aliases used by the bloated baby farmer. Arrested with Mrs Dyer was her son-in-law, a Mr Arthur Palmer, who happened to be living with her at the time. Also in the house were two children, no doubt lucky to be alive, as Mrs Dyer usually despatched her charges within a few hours of receiving them. They were Ellen Oliver, a girl who had arrived from Plymouth, and a boy whose name would seem to differ in various reports. In most he is reported as Harry Symmonds, but in others he is called Willie Thornton. He was nine years old and able to provide police with vital evidence. Also in residence, but apparently out when the police arrived, was Mrs Dyer's daughter, Polly, and *her* daughter, only a baby.

Mrs Dyer was lodged in Reading Gaol, where she made two abortive attempts at suicide, the first with a pair of scissors with which she tried to stab herself; thwarted, she then tried to strangle herself with her boot laces, with no greater success.

When the trial opened, Mrs Dyer was charged with the murder of little Edith Marmon, one of the only two bodies to be identified, the other being that of a small boy named Simonds. His mother could not be traced, but the tiny corpse was recognised by a lady who had looked after him for some time, before she, as many others, had done before her, had innocently replied to Mrs Dyer's advertisement, disguised by the *nom de plume* Mrs Thomas.

The case was soon dropped against Arthur Palmer through lack of evidence. If he was not involved, then he must have been incredibly naive. His evidence was to help place Mrs Dyer on the scaffold, as was his wife Polly's, who testified that her mother had at times visited her with various small children who seemed to disappear overnight.

Polly said her mother once visited her with a child in a pram. 'She had stayed the night and left in the morning with no child, but a brown paper parcel under her arm. By this time the trial of Mrs Dyer had moved to the Old Bailey.

More damning evidence came from the small survivor, Harry Symmonds. He remembered about twenty-five young children coming and going to the house in Reading. By this time the enormity of the situation was beginning to dawn upon an outraged public. They were out for Mrs Dyer's blood. The sight in the crowded courtroom of Evalina Marmon weeping over her murdered child incensed them and the evidence of the other witnesses, sensationalised by the media, worked up public hysteria.

Reports were coming from all over the country of different children who had been adopted by this kindly old lady. More damning evidence came from Polly, who said she had seen her mother in Cardiff about a year previously with three children, and a day later had seen her without any. None of those children was ever traced.

Harry Symmonds gave evidence that the carpet bag holding one of the tiny bodies found in Clapper's Pool was the one he had brought to Mrs Dyer's house.

Granny Smith, a neighbour of Mrs Dyer in Reading, swore that a brick found holding down one of the tiny cadavers was the same one that Mrs Dyer used to keep her flat irons on.

Mrs Gibbs, the matron of Reading Gaol, produced a written confession the baby farmer composed in custody.

A woman called Charlotte Culham gave evidence that she had often seen Mrs Dyer with small children, and also seen her with packages that resembled the bodies of small children.

It also came to light that Mrs Dyer was a close friend of another convicted baby farmer, Margaret Waters.

With such evidence against her, the gross and wimpering woman could do nothing more than plead guilty but insane. The insanity claim she hoped would be endorsed by the fact that she had spent several brief periods in mental institutions in Wells and Gloucester. However, the jury were having none of it; she had entered these institutions of her own volition, possibly when the police were getting a little too close to her activities in that part of the country.

Mrs Amelia Elizabeth Dyer was found guilty and sentenced to hang. The execution was carried out on 10 June 1896 at Newgate. The biggest concern of the executioner, a man named Billington, was that the now quivering bulk of a fifteen stone woman would snap her head off as the rope took up the slack on the trip through the trapdoor. Billington, however, was a master of his trade and fixed the arms with ropes so that they would absorb some of the shock.

Thus ends the story of Reading's most notorious citizen.

MRS DYER'S HOUSE AT 45 KENSINGTON ROAD, READING.

READING BOROUGH BENCH.—SATURDAY.

ore Mr F. B. Parfitt (in the chair), and Mr H. M. Wallis.

THE CHILD MURDER.

WOMAN ARRESTED.

anie Dyer, *alias* Thomas, an elderly woman, of 45, nsington Road, Reading, described as a nurse, was rged with having, on or about the 20th March, 1896, ne parish of St. Mary, feloniously killed and murdered ild unknown

uperintendent Tewsley said that on Monday last a cel was found in the Thames, and when it was opened was found to contain the body of a female d. By means of the address on the parcel prisoner was traced to 45, Kensington Road, the ress given on the parcel. They had evidence to re that the prisoner took out a brown paper parcel Monday, and that she borrowed some string. The ng around the parcel was identical with the string borrowed, and the tape round the child's neck esponds with the tape found at the prisoner's house. should like to have a remand for a week. The ndant had a husband, but he was not living with They were strangers to this part of the country.

reply to the Bench, prisoner said, "I do not know thing about it; it is all a mystery to me."

he prisoner was remanded to Saturday.

RUNKENNESS.—Wm. Frewin, of 60, Essex Street, labourer, charged with being drunk whilst in charge of a horse and in King's Road on April 2 P.C. Harry Scotcher proved case.—P.S. Connoh deposed that the defendant used dis- ing language in the police station.—A fine of 10s and , or ten days' hard labour, was imposed.

orge Sumpter, of Three-mile-cross, was charged with drunk and committing a nuisance in the Basingstoke on April 2.—The defendant pleaded guilty, and was fined r five days' hard labour. P.C. Martin gave evidence.

SAULT.—Alfred Shepherd, of 14, Boarded Lane, labourer, charged with unlawfully assaulting Henry Bentley, a police table, whilst in the execution of his duty on the previous .—P.C. Bentley said that about ten o'clock he was in d Street and heard a whistle blow. He proceeded to St. 's Butts and saw two men fighting. He endeavoured to rate them. He took one man into custody, when the ndant came up to him, and said with an oath that he was oing to take him into custody. The defendant then dealt blow on the chest, and then with the other hand struck again. Witness was hustled considerably by the crowd, e at length got the prisoner to the police station.—The dant said he was very sorry.—The Chairman remarked the police must be protected. The defendant would be 40s, or twenty-one days' hard labour.

OTBALL IN THE STREETS. William Clark, a lad, pleaded to playing football in Howard Street, on March 22.—D.C. rson said the defendant was playing with other lads. They had several complaints of boys playing football in the s in this locality.—The boy was discharged with a caution.

MRS DYER'S ARREST, AND ANOTHER BODY IS IDENTIFIED.

THE ALLEGED ATTEMPTED SUICIDE.

As many exaggerated statements have been circulated with regard to the alleged attempted suicide of the woman Dyer, a true statement of the affair will be read with interest. The prisoner was apprehended on the evening of Good Friday and brought to the police office. While the charge was being written, and the woman-searcher sent for, she sat in the charge-office in a chair with a police-sergeant by her side. While in this position she took a pair of scissors from her pocket, but before she had time to do herself any harm, presuming that was her intention, they were wrested from her by the police-sergeant. She remained quiet for a few minutes, but presently she was noticed to take a lace from her boot and put it round her neck, but it was at once taken possession of. The statement that she tied the lace in a knot, and that the knot came precisely in the same place on her neck, viz., under the left ear, as where the tape round the children's necks was tied, is all imagination.

ANOTHER BODY IDENTIFIED.

BRICK AND CLOTHES ALSO RECOGNISED.

We are able to inform our readers that on Wednesday a third body was identified. It was that of the first child found, and was picked up out of the water near the Kennet's mouth on March 30, and it has been identified as that of the child of a woman who was confined in St. Paul's, Bristol. The woman was single, and a domestic servant. The description given by the woman tallies exactly with the child, and there can be no doubt the infant picked up is her child. The baby, who, by the way, was described by Mr O. C. Maurice as being between twelve and eighteen months old, came into Mrs Dyer's possession in the usual way. She put an advertisement in the *Bristol Daily Press* in the common form, adopting the *alias* of Thornley. The mother answered the advertisement, and on March 5 the prisoner Dyer went to Bristol for the child, receiving £10, and also her railway fare. She left for Reading by the 5.50 train, with the child, the same evening. The woman, whom the mother has since identified in Reading Gaol as Mrs Dyer, promised to give the little one a good home. The same evening a neighbour of Mrs Dyer's saw her enter the house in Kensington-road with the child, and Mrs Dyer said she had taken it in to nurse for a few weeks as the mother had just died. The child was seen in the house several times after this by other persons. Curiously enough, it was not despatched to its watery grave till the morning of the day on which it was found. The body appears to have been wrapped up in the piece of brown paper which she had received from Bristol, in October, and placed in the kitchen cupboard. We have already referred to the complaint which Mrs Chandler, who came to lodge with Mrs Dyer in February, made of a bad smell in the house, but it also appears that the

FOLLY CROSSROADS, SCENE OF TWO POLICEMEN'S MURDERS.

PC WILLIAM GOLBY DISCOVERED HIS COLLEAGUE'S BODY.

Death on Duty at Hungerford

At 9.30pm on 11 December 1876, PC Isaacs of Hungerford Police Station chatted with Inspector Joseph Drewitt outside the Red Lion, a well known hostelry. After a few minutes' pleasantries, they parted company, Isaacs to continue his beat, and Inspector Drewitt for another conference point with young PC Shorter, at Folly Crossroads, less than a mile to the north of the town.

As Isaacs continued around Hungerford's narrow streets, he heard the crack of gunfire, at about 9.50. The sound was far off and barely audible. Little did the young policeman know that he was not to see either of his colleagues alive again.

At 10pm PC Golby, also of Hungerford Police Station,proceeded to the Bear Inn in the centre of the town, where he was to meet Drewitt. When, after some twenty minutes, the Inspector had failed to arrive, Golby set off in the direction from which he anticipated Drewitt would appear, after his meet with PC Shorter at the turnpike at Folly Crossroads.

As Golby passed the turnpike gate, he noticed what seemed to be a pile of rags beside the road. On closer examination the constable found the body of his colleague, PC Shorter. The corpse was barely recognisable, the face battered with extreme savagery, the skull smashed to such an extent that much of the brain was some two feet away.

PC Golby, still in a state of shock and incredulity, ran the few yards to the turnpike cottage. He told the gatekeeper to keep vigil while he went back to the station for assistance. Word was also sent to the Superintendent of Newbury to arrange for Shorter's body to be moved. Golby returned later with other officers to search the surrounding area, but it was not until the following morning that the terribly mutilated body of Inspector Joseph Drewitt was discovered.

It was in the hedgerow less than twenty yards from that of Constable Shorter. The Inspector had been shot behind the ear at close range, but according to later medical reports, this had not killed the unusually strong policeman. The cause of death had been the terrible bludgeoning he had received from a blunt instrument.

The neighbourhood was apalled at the atrocities perpetrated on two popular local policemen. Both left widows; Drewitt also left five sorrowing children. An outraged public demanded swift justice and retribution. Their wishes were met.

By 9am the following morning, four local poachers were in custody. William Day, aged 39, and the Tidbury brothers — Henry, aged 26, William, aged 24, and Francis, aged 17. They had all been seen in the vicinity of the turnpike and the nearby Duncan Woods.

Superintendent Bennet from Newbury, accompanied by Sergeant Bull, had found a hiking stick belonging to Henry Tidbury near the scene of the crimes. There was also a distinctive tobacco box thought to belong to William Day.

When the Superintendent and Sergeant Bull called on William Day, he denied that the tobacco box was his. Dr Major, a police physician, found Day's trousers smothered with red lead, thereby completely obliterating any sign of blood. Day was cautioned and arrested. A similar story emerged at William Tidbury's house. He claimed to have been painting; he also had trousers soaked in red lead.

Footprints matching the shoes of the other two brothers, Henry and Francis, were found in the vicinity of the crime. All three Tidburys were cautioned and arrested.

With the prisoners lodged at various police stations, Day and William Tidbury in Newbury, and Henry and Francis in Reading, evidence began to flood in.

The small court at Reading was inundated with spectators as various witnesses gave their accounts. The prisoners were brought in by train to tumultuous shouts of revenge.

Bill Williams, a journeyman, witnessed how he had met Day in the Barley Mow at Hungerford, and sold him the incriminating tobacco box.

The landlord of the Oxford Arms, a pub near Duncan Woods, stated that he heard a gunshot at the appropriate time.

Blood had been found on the clothing of Henry and Francis Tidbury.

The Stocks of two guns were found at Eddington Hill, near Hungerford. They were thought to have been used in the death of Inspector Drewitt, firstly to shoot him and then to batter him.

William Bailey, an engine driver, said he recognised one of the guns as one he had sold to Henry Tidbury.

A man named William Talbot also claimed he sold the second gun to Henry.

Henry Jones, a game-keeper, identified ferret lines found in Duncan Woods as belonging to both Day and the Tidburys.

At this point Mr G. C. Cherry, presiding, adjourned the proceedings to Reading Assizes.

The Assizes opened in mid-February, 1877. The three Tidbury brothers and William Day were accused of both murders. The outcome seemed a foregone conclusion.

After much of the previous evidence had been repeated, Professor Tidy, a police forensic expert, stated that after detailed examination he had found human blood on all three of the Tidburys' clothing. Damning evidence indeed.

When Professor Tidy sat down, worse was to come for the defendants, as a plethora of witnesses placed every permutation of the four in or about the vicinity at various times that evening.

Later forensic evidence was also to prove that one of the stocks of Henry Tidburn's shotguns fitted exactly the pattern of marks found on PC Shorter's helmet.

The evidence was overwhelming, but none so precise and clear as that given by a Mr Bryant and his teenage daughter. They had arrived home near the turnpike crossroads at 10.15pm, they had heard a shot at 10.25, and they had seen William Tidbury and William Day leaving a path near the woods at 10.50, which was some five minutes after PC Golby had discovered the first body.

On 19 February, at Reading Assizes, before Mr Justice Lindley, the four accused were called to give evidence.

William Tidbury stated that on 11 December he had been working until late at a local farm (this had already been borne out by the farmer). Leaving at about 10.30, he had walked back to Hungerford by a wide track that skirted Duncan Woods, by way of the turnpike crossroads. At about 10.45 he had met William Day, who had also been working late, and they had travelled together to their appropriate homes, the houses being a stone's throw from each other. They had chatted by his front gate before retiring. In answer to a prosecution question, he stated that he did hear indistinct gunfire, but had thought no more of it. He could not explain the bloodstains on his trousers, but he strongly suspected them to be rabbit's blood. He fervently denied that he had been at the scene of the murders or had been in any way involved.

In quick succession, the remaining two brothers were called to the stand. Henry, morose, defiant and all but monosyllabic, had been out for a drink early in the evening, but had returned before nine with his younger brother, Francis, with whom he shared a small cottage. He had not shot or bludgeoned anybody; his guns had been stolen and the stick was not his. His counsel had tried to disprove the footprint evidence as indistinct and he vehemently denied that he had ever used a hiking stick. Henry returned to his seat with an arrogant shrug of his shoulders.

When 17-year-old Francis took the stand, he unconvincingly tried to adopt his elder brother's aggressive contempt for authority, but the nights in prison and the unyielding crowds accompanying him and his brothers wherever they went had adversely affected the young man. Blood being thicker than water, he repeated, word for faltering word, everything his brother Henry had stated. He was clever enough to realise that he was defending the indefensible.

When Francis finished his evidence, it was William Day's turn. He calmly and resolutely took the oath. His story was long and detailed.

William Day had been working late at a nearby farm. This was verified by the farmer. Leaving at about 10.30, he had approached the turnpike at Folly Lane Junction near Duncan Woods, from the east. It was about 10.45 when he met William Tidbury on the large track or roadway that skirts the woods. William was leaning against a tree. There was no sign of the other brothers. He noticed a dark bulk lying a few yards back along the causeway. 'What is that?' he enquired.

'It is only a drunk,' replied William Tidbury. 'Let us get along home now, Bill.'

William Day stated that he had made towards the shadow, but Tidbury had barred his way and ushered him towards home. A few minutes later they had acknowledged Mr Bryant and his daughter outside their house, and then trudged home and stood chatting for some time on the doorstep.

In answer to a question from the prosecution, Day replied that William Tidbury seemed very much on edge and in a nervous condition, which was unusual for him.

Day stated that in the early hours of the morning he had been awakened by Henry and Francis Tidbury. They warned him with veiled threats against mentioning anything that he had witnessed the previous night.

When questioned about the tobacco box, Day admitted that he had regularly, and recently, poached and snared in Duncan Woods, and it was more than probably that he had dropped it then.

After a long interrogation from the prosecution, Day was asked to sit down.

William Day's controversial story gained support from an unexpected source — PC Butcher, a constable at Newbury. He had heard a heated exchange between Day and William Tidbury while they were in custody at Newbury. They were unaware that they were within earshot of the constable.

PC Butcher referred to his notes. Day and Tidbury had met in the toilet. William Day sounded frustrated.

'I'm not swinging for your two crazy brothers, Bill. I wasn't there at the time and I'm damned if they're going to top me for your brothers. They're no bloody relations of mine. If you want to, that's down to you but I'm blowing the gaff. I'm not taking the bloody drop for them.'

PC Butcher stated that while this heated exchange was going on, the only words spoken by Tidbury were, 'Shoosh, Bill, someone will hear you. Everything will be alright.'

The constable said that then there was silence and the two prisoners were returned to their respective cells.

Both prosecution and defence lawyers gave eloquent closing speeches. It seemed the weight of evidence had come down substantially and significantly for the Crown case.

There was, however, a niggling doubt in the minds of some of the jurors. Had all four defendants committed the brutal crimes, or had just two of the brother perpetrated these heinous events, later to be joined by William who had done his best to abet them after the event? Had William Day, a man with a long criminal record, just happened along inadvertently?

There would seem to have been little doubt, however, in Mr Justice Lindley's mind. After a long and colourful summing up, in which he swelt on the viciousness of the attack and the grievousness of the wounds, the callousness of the defendants and the misery of the surviving relatives, he made one adamant point.

'Ask yourselves,' he questioned the jury, 'is it possible that two exceptionally strong and stalwart officers could be put to death so easily by just one man and a mere youth, or would it have taken at least three if not four men to overcome them and cause such severe injuries?'

Here he finished his summing up and the jury retired.

They returned two hours later, when the foreman addressed the hushed courtroom with their unanimous verdicts.

William Day: Not guilty of the murder of Inspector Drewitt or PC Shorter.

William Tidbury: Not guilty of the murder of Inspector Drewitt or PC Shorter, but guilty of aiding and abetting others in both cases.

Henry Tidbury: Guilty of both the murder of Inspector Drewitt and PC Shorter.

Francis Tidbury: Guilty of both the murders of Inspector Drewitt and PC Shorter, but with a strong plea for leniency because of his youth.

The court was stunned. Justice Lindley looked stern and dissatisfied. He acquitted two men and then placed the black cap on his head and sentenced the other two to death. He then explained that William Tidbury could not be convicted of aiding and abetting because he had not been charged with that crime.

Two men walked thankfully and possibly a little luckily from court; the other two dejectedly to their cells.

Francis Tidbury received a certain amount of sympathy over the following few days, but the public were so outraged at the brutality involved, it carried little weight. Public sympathy was more inclined towards the fatherless children and widows. A massive collection was made in local towns, and two crosses were erected close to where the men met their tragic ends.

Francis Tidbury admitted his guilt from his death cell, but stated that he had been attacked by the police and had killed in self-defence. This of course, was quite ridiculous, as neither of the officers' truncheons had been drawn from their cases. This suggested they had been attacked one at a time, and taken by surprise, which reinforced the verdict that two and not four men were involved.

Henry Tidbury admitted the crime in a letter from his cell. He also apologised to his brother, William, and Bill Day, and stated that as God was his judge, they were never involved.

At Reading Gaol, at precisely 8am on 12 March executioner Marwood did his duty, and Henry and Francis Tidbury met their Maker.

The *Reading Observer* described the hanging in graphic detail, even to the description of the corpses. 'The bodies were cut down at 9am precisely and then the jury proceeded to the execution room to view the bodies. The deceased looked livid and their necks appeared to have been broken.'

PC THOMAS SHORTER.

INSPECTOR JOSEPH DREWITT.

THE MEMORIAL TO INSPECTOR DREWITT: PC SHORTER'S MEMORIAL IS NEARBY.

THE 19TH CENTURY READING GAOL WHERE WILDE AND WOOLRIDGE LANGUISHED.

OSCAR WILDE TOLD THE TALE OF TROOPER WOOLRIDGE.

TROOPS PARADE IN WOOLRIDGE'S WINDSOR — IN PEASCOD STREET. (RS)

A Clewer Crime of Passion

Oscar Wilde's *Ballad of Reading Gaol* tells of the hanging of a trooper at the prison:

'And all men kill the thing they love
By all let this be heard
Some do it with a bitter look
Some with a flattering word
The coward does it with a kiss
The brave man with a sword.'

Wilde portrays a romantic young man who killed his wife in passion and then paid the ultimate penalty.

But who was the young trooper? And was it really the crime of passion that Wilde eloquently records? Wilde took poetic licence to the extreme, for the true story is much more down to earth. Itis,in fact, a tale of jealousy, mistrust and uncontrollable temper.

In 1896, Charles T. Woolridge had been a serving trooper with the Royal Horse Guards for ten years. He was a good soldier, but his marriage was on the rocks. Woolridge and his wife, Laura, were living apart. It was rumoured that Laura had an eye for the men, which did nothing to consolidate the marriage, or to abate Woolridge's white-hot temper, which was never far away. They had decided on a trial separation, Charles staying with his friends at barracks in London, while his wife lived at Alma Terrace, Arthur Road, Clewer, a district of Windsor.

Laura shared rooms in the small terraced house with Alice Cox, a young lady who worked with her at a local Post Office.

How much of Laura's promiscuity was fact, and what only existed in Woolridge's overactive imagination, we shall never know. Alice Cox was later to swear on oath that, for the three years she hadknown Laura, she was only visited by one man other than Charles. He was Robert Harvey, a corporal in the Guards. Alice swore that he only took tea once, and certainly did not stay overnight.

Be that as it may, Woolridge had his suspicions. He would call at the house at random times to see if he could catch his wife in compromising circumstances. He suspected a young lawyer, a man whose name never came to light, even in the subsequent trial.

Whenever Woolridge did call on his wife, a violent row ensued. Volleys of accusations were fired from both sides. On 16 March they culminated in Woolridge punching his wife repeatedly in the face, blacking her eyes and making hernose bleed, hardly the romantic young soldier of Wilde's ballad.

After this brutal episode, Woolridge returned to his barracks. There he composed his wife a letter (later found among Laura's belongings by PC Myers). It stated the soldier's undying love for his wife but also made it plain that he realised that they could not live in harmony, so they had better not see each other. Woolridge swore that he would not visit her at Windsor again, unfortunately an oath that he failed to keep.

Charles Woolridge had sent messages to his wife arranging a date in London. When she did not arrive, he presented himself at Alma Terrace the following morning. It was 9 o'clock on 29 March, when Alice Cox let him in. He asked to see Laura, but was told that she had no wish to see him. Finally, to avoid a scene, his wife granted him an audience and Alice returned to her room upstairs to allow them some privacy.

Minutes later the inevitable argument erupted. Alice heard Laura scream, then the slamming of the front door, followed by a second scream from the roadway.

She dashed out into the road, where she saw Laura's inert and profusely bleeding body by the side of the carriageway. Woolridge was nowhere to be seen. Alice was instantly joined by Fred Davis, a neighbouring tailor. Together they turned Laura over. Her throat had been slashed viciously, and she must have died almost instantaneously. More neighbours arrived, aroused by the frantic screaming. The police were summoned.

At 9.20, PC Foster was filling in reports at the Police Station, Windsor. The officer looked up from his desk to see Trooper C. T. Woolridge standing there. The soldier was calm and spoke deliberately. 'I have killed my wife,' he stated, 'I have slit her throat. She was carrying on with some lawyer.'

There was little more said. P.C. Foster took down the relevant particulars and then escorted Woolridge to the cells.

At his subsequent trial, Charles Woolridge was to take the contradictory step of pleading not guilty, but the outcome was a foregone conclusion; he was unanimously convicted.

There was an eloquent and impassioned speech from Mr Wash, Woolridge's defence lawyer. He took Wilde's viewpoint of the young man in love, and a spontaneous killing by a man whose passion exploded through a short-fused temper.

The prosecution pointed out, quite correctly, that Woolridge had borrowed the razor from a fellow trooper in London the day before he travelled to Windsor. There had therefore been a certain amount of premeditation.

Mr Justice Hawkins, in his summing up, certainly had little sympathy for Woolridge. He informed a hushed court that, even if the trooper's wife was 'playing around', that was no excuse for murder, premeditated or spontaneous.

The unanimous verdict was 'guilty'. The judge sentenced the trooper to death.

Woolridge seemed unconcerned. He met his sentence smiling and waving to his friends. Probably life without Laura meant little to him anyway. He was led from the court in good spirits.

It was reported that, while incarcerated at Reading's morbid gaol, Woolridge once again affirmed his guilt, and formally stated that he accepted his terminal punishment as the logical outcome.

He walked to his death at Reading on 7 July 1896, the famous hangman Billington in charge of operations. He later announced that Woolridge went to his death with great courage.

'The brave man had killed the thing he loved,' if not with a sword, at least with a razor.

TROOPER WOOLRIDGE TRAVELLED FROM LONDON ON THAT FATEFUL DAY IN 1896; THE GWR STATION. (CB)

A POLICEMAN PAUSES IN PEASCOD STREET, WINDSOR, WHERE SHILL'S LANDLADY SOUGHT HELP. (RS)

The Missing Wife of Windsor

Jane Holt was an attractive, level-headedwoman in her late sixties. Her second husband had died some years before, and now she lived with her son, George Grimsdale and his two young children in a large house at Windsor — 37 Victoria Cottages.

It was Friday 19 December 1884, and Mrs Holt was walking swiftly in search of a policeman. She was not quite sure what she was going to tell him when she found one. It was just a strange feeling and of course the inability to contact anyone in the Shill's room.

Maria Shill had taken the room at George Grimsdale's house in mid-November, with her three young children. She was dark-haired and slim, 32 years of age and pleasant. Her husband, Joseph, had moved in a fortnight later. He was a tailor by trade, miserably jealous and, Jane Holt had decided, extremely violent. He was thirty-four, but looked much older, had a grotesquely humped back, a grey beard and droopy moustache.

Jane had heard sounds of violence coming from the Shill's room on several occasions, and she knew that in early October, shortly before their arrival, Maria had complained to the police after sustaining a broken collar bone when Joseph pushed her through a window.

It was this and the suspiciously silent room that initiated Jane Holt's search for a police officer.

As she walked, Jane reflected on some of the curious happenings of the day. She had taken the Shills' two older children, a boy and a girl aged six and four, for a Christmas treat, along with her two grandchildren, had then gone shopping to enjoy the festive lights of Windsor. The youngest child, a mere toddler, had stayed with her parents at 37 Victoria Cottages. The little mite had objected strongly. She knew she was missing something, even if she did not know quite what, but she and her parents had returned to their large room at the base of the Grimsdale's house.

On their return, Mrs Holt and the children had tried unsuccessfully to get a reaction with persistent knocking at the Shill's door.

The more Jane Holt mulled things over in her mind, the less cause there seemed to be for alarm. She was beginning to have second thoughts about bothering the police with such a mass of suspicion based on such little tangible fact.

Then, as she turned into Peascod Street and neared the local police station, she initially decided to turn round and head for home. She reasoned that, if the Shills wished not to be disturbed, it was no business of hers or indeed of the police.

At 9pm on Friday 19 December, PC Laney left the police station to begin his patrol. He had only walked a few yards when he noticed an elderly lady approaching him in a somewhat hesitant manner. He approached her and asked if he could help.

In the somewhat hesitant speech of someone afraid of causing embarrassment, Mrs Jane Holt explained her concern at the reluctance of the Shills to answer their door.

PC Laney, accompanied by Mrs Holt, returned to Victoria Cottages. There they were met by her son, George Grimsdale, her two grandchildren, the elder two Shill children and two neighbours, Hardwicke Davies and John Thompson, who lodged in the adjoining house.

PC Laney knocked on the Shill's door. This time there was evidence of occupation — the thin, reed-like sound of a young child's voice and the discernibly laboured breathing of a man in deep slumber.

The small party returned to the outside of the house where, with the help of a bricklayer's trowel, PC Laney raised the casement some ten or twelve inches. He shone his torch inside and sawnothing amiss. The dark room was untidy, a large bundle of clothes lay near the wardrobe door, on the bed lay the misshapen form of the Windsor tailor and next to him sat the figure of his youngest daughter. Of Maria Shill, there was no sign.

The two neighbours held the casement, and PC Laney reached in with a broomhandle and pushed Joseph Shill on the leg. There was little reaction, as Shill partially awoke, turned over, snorted and then returned to his deep sleep. It was the slumber of a man who had been at his cups for some considerable time.

There seemed little more to do. Grimsdale's daughter, a lass of about twelve, was squeezed through the opening to retrieve the toddler and pass her out. She, with her brother and sister, slept that night with the Grimsdale family, a not unusual occurrence.

PC Laney made a brief note, and then returned to his tour of duty.

Saturday morning, 20 December was a worrying time for Jane Holt. She had not slept much the night before; she was worried, and she was curious about her tenants. She had been up since six, but respect for the Shills' priacy had made her refrain from enquiring until 9.30. Then at last she knocked loudly on the door.

The gruff voice of Joseph Shill answered.

'Have you had breakfast?' enquired Mrs Holt.

'No,' was the curt reply.

'Can you put some food out for the children? I gave them supper last night,' Jane glanced at the five tousled heads in various parts of the living room.

'I shall get them some food later,' replied Shill, from behind the closed door.

Jane Holt breathed in deeply. 'Have you seen you wife, Mr Shill?'

'No.' Jane Holt waited but Shill did not elaborate. She left the house to do some errands.

She returned some half an hour later to find the Shill's bedroom door open and Joseph gone. He had however, left food out for the children.

Neither Joseph, nor his wife, Maria, were seen again that day. Grimsdale's eldest daughter cleaned the room briefly with a broom and the rest of the children scurried about the house.

There was another worried elderly lady on 20 December 1884. It was Mrs Prime, Maria Shill's mother. She had disapproved of Shill from the start. She dearly wished that her only daughter had settled down with Les Williams, a hardworking friend of her son. What Maria had seen in the humpbacked and dreary little tailor she would never know. Also she knew Shill to be a toper and, when in his cups, a man of violence. Bruises on Maria were pronounced and regular proof of assaults, culminating in the broken collar bone of the previous October.

What added considerably to this worried mother's concern was a letter she had received that morning. It was from Joseph. In a few lines, just a little more than a note, he had told her that Maria was depressed. He had not seen her for a while and he was pretty sure she had committed suicide.

One can imagine the effect this had on an elderly mother. Her concern changed to panic. She contacted her eldest son, William and, accompanied by her younger son and Les Williams, they travelled across town to 37 Victoria Cottages.

George Grimsdale greeted Maria's anxious family politely and courteously, and answered their questions frankly.

Yes, the children were well, as they could see. No,he did not know where Maria was. He had not seen her since early Friday morning. No, Joseph Shill was not at home. No, they could not inspect his room unless Joseph was present. No, he did not know where he was. The best thing they could do was comb the hundreds of pubs in the area.

William Prime thanked Grimsdale politely and the small band of disappointed people walked dejectedly away.

Joseph Shill returned home in the early hours of Sunday 21 December. He slept deeply until around 9.30, when he arose, breakfasted, and took his children out for a walk. He returned at 11.30, and deposited his children with Jane Holt. In reply to yet another question from the impromptu baby-sitter, he said that he did not know where his wife was, but he did believe that poor Maria had left him.

Sunday lunchtime found Joseph Shill bent over a table at the King's Head at Egham. He was drinking his Sunday lunch. As he sat morosely contemplating, he was startled by a large fist hammering the table. He looked up to see the worried face of William Prime staring down at him. William was accompanied by his brother and Les Williams.

'Where is Maria?' William threatened. 'Have you hurt her, you humpbacked bastard?'

'I do believe,' Shill started unsteadily, 'that our beloved Maria has committed suicide.'

'Suicide,' screamed Les, 'you've killed her, you drunken bastard.'

Williams jumped at the tailor, striking him repeatedly with blows to the head. Left and right hooks followed each other until the frightened tailor sank to the floor.

Williams was grabbed and restrained by half a dozen regulars until he and the Prime brothers were ejected into Egham's busy streets.

Late on Sunday evening, William Prime could stand the pressure no more. He called at the police station in central Windsor. He explained to the desk sergeant that he was worried that his sister had been murdered by her husband, Joseph Shill. The desk sergeant contacted Superintendent Misty Hayes and a missing person enquiry commenced.

On Monday 22 December, George Grimsdale found himself under pressure. His motherhad nagged him for some time about entering his lodger's room. George had reasoned with her, explaining that his daughter had swept the room two days ago, and found nothing. Also, he explained that, to his knowledge, Joseph Shill had committed no crime, and his tenants were entitled to their privacy. Finally he pointed out to his mother that there were but two keys to the room and the Shills had one each.

Jane Holt insisted, her son resisted. Jane Holt persisted, her son protested. Jane Holt persevered and her son capitulated. He walked to his tool shed and came back with a garden spade.

He forced the door and entered the room. It seemed untidy, but that was quite normal. He opened cupboards and drawers, and found nothing suspicious. He bent down and pulled a large rolled-up blanket from under the bed. It unrolled as he tugged it across the bedroom floor, and inside was the blood-soaked corpse of Maria Shill.

White-faced, George Grimsdale turned to his mother. 'Touch nothing', he shouted as he sped towards the police station. George Grimsdale returned within thirty minutes, accompanied by PC May and a coroner's clerk. Already the house was surrounded by inquisitive people. PC Maydid little but keep back the crowds and briefly interview Mrs Holt and George Grimsdale.

May was shortly joined by Superintendent Hayes and the local police doctor, an astute man named Edward Stacey Norris. Norris inspected the body and determined the cause of death. There were six deep and severe scalp wounds. Maria's demise was certainly caused by a massive haemorrhage of the brain.

Hayes found the murder weapon, a flat iron with blood and Maria's hair upon it, in a cupboard. The fire fender where the young wife had fallen was besmirched with blood, and a pair of Joseph Shill's shoes were found drenched with it.

Superintendent Hayes sealed the bedroom, leaving PC May at the house until Norris had arranged for the body to go to the mortuary.

Inspector Collis and Sergeant Fleet of the Surrey Police made their way through the streets of Egham to a rather down-market area known as Fishers Fields. They had had a message from Windsor, and were on their way to arrest Joseph Shill. They had heard that Shill had been seen with a local man, Johnny Turner, at the King's Head Monday lunchtime. It was now the evening, and the officers approached Turner's house.

Sergeant Fleet knocked on the door. Ashe opened it, the owner seemed almost to expect them. He invited them in and, as they crossed the threshold, a small dishevelled hunchback made his faltering way towards them.

'Joseph Shill, I am arresting you for the murder of your wife, Maria Shill, at Windsor, on 19th December.'

'My wife?' answered a stunned Shill, 'My wife dead? I haven't seen my darling Maria since Friday.'

Nothing more was said as the small tailor was accompanied to Egham Police Station and subsequently to Windsor.

Shill was charged briefly at Windsor Petty Sessions on 5 January 1885. He was remanded in custody until the February assizes.

At the assizes the evidence against him was overwhelming. Prosecution solicitors, Messrs Greene and Cowper, had done their groundwork well. Jane Holt's, Grimsdale's and police evidence all pointed strongly to the tailor's guilt. Apart from the evidence of bloodstained items such as the fender, the flat iron and the shoes, the Surrey Police had retrieved a pair of Shill's bloodstained trousers from John Turner's house.

Mr Darling, a court solicitor allotted to Shill, did his best to substantiate his not guilty plea. Would a guilty man leave such bloodstained, incriminating evidence about the house for three days? he enquired of the jury. Would he not clear up and then be off as quickly as possible? Could any man sleep for three nights on a bed with the bloodstained body of his wife beneath it?

Darling's points were credible in the circumstances; the only plausible explanation of Shill's actions after the crime was that he was in a drunken stupor.

Shill's suggestion that his wife committed suicide was dashed by the evidence of Dr Norris, who insisted that most of the head injuries would have been impossible to achieve by someone attempting suicide and that,in the annals of crime, he had yet to hear of a case where a person attempted suicide by bashing his head with a flat iron. It seemed a singularly unlikely mode of achieving one's objective.

It was suggested, slightly to the embarrassment of PC Laney, that the bundle of clothes lying by the wardrobe, that was illuminated by the officer's torch on Friday the 19th, was, in all probability, the lifeless body of the unfortunate Maria. PC Laney grudgingly admitted this was probably so.

The case was tolerably brief and onesided. The Judge's summing-up left only one possible verdict.

The jury retired at 5.50, and returned with a unanimous verdict at 6.35 — 'guilty!'

THE TRANQUIL THAMES AT EGHAM, WHERE THE PRIME BROTHERS AND LES WILLIAMS SQUARED UP TO JOSEPH SHILL. (CB)

SHILL MET HIS DESTINY AT THE ASSIZES. WINDSOR'S GUILDHALL PROVIDED THE COURTROOM; DRAWN HERE ONE YEAR LATER. (RS)

OLD WATCHFIELD IS LITTLE CHANGED SINCE THE CARTER KILLING.

WATCHFIELD'S WIFE-KILLER

At 11.00pm on 20 July 1893, nine-year-old Thomas Carter was awoken by a turbulent row in the room below his. Thomas and his five-year-old brother slept in one of two small bedrooms in a small farmhouse which joined a terraced street in the tiny hamlet of Watchfield, Berkshire.

He could hear the loud yet muffled interchanges between his father, John Carter, and his stepmother of only a few months, Rhoda. They had quarrelled little since she had come to live with them in March, but he knew his father to be a man of violent temper, and Rhoda to have a mean and verbally savage streak within her.

The row below dulled and then flickered to life, muted for a short while and then raised into a furious crescendo. There was the sound of striking flesh upon flesh, and then the distinct cry from Rhoda; 'No John, no,' then almost beseechingly, 'The Lord have mercy on me.' Then there was silence.

Young Thomas Carter was woken again at 4.30am that morning by his father. This was not unusual as the Carters were farmers and it was Thomas's duty to herd the cows. As he sat there breakfasting with his younger brother, he watched his father busying himself in an unusual way. He was taking firewood and a large cauldron into the smithy that adjoined the cottage. This in its turn adjoined the stables and the barn. Not seeing the significance at the time of the two articles, or of the prong (pitchfork) and shovel that followed them, the two boys finished their frugal breakfast and set out upon their chores.

Mrs Titcombe, Rhoda's mother, lived with her son less than fifty yards from Carter in the same street. It was her habit to drop in and see her daughter most mornings, and to take tea and chatter, a habit that John Carter frowned upon, as it interrupted Rhoda in her household duties.

At 9am on 21 July she knocked at the door. She had not seen her daughter since 9 o'clock the previous evening. Mrs Titcombe got no reply. Peering through the kitchen window she could see the remains of three breakfasts and her daughter's new green coat hanging on the back of the kitchen door.

When she turned to go, she saw Carter emerging from the smithy. He looked stunned, almost in a trance, but he soon regained his composure. He locked the door of the smithy behind him, and then sauntered towards his mother-in-law. He stood there, a rough-cast, raw boned, slightly menacing man.

'Where is Rhoda?' enquired Mrs Titcombe.

'Gone to see her sister at Eastleech,' came the reply.

'Oh, she didn't say anything to me.' Mrs Titcombe was already suspicious. She didn't like John Carter. Rhoda, at thirty, was his third wife, some seventeen years younger than him.

'Can I do anything for you, John? Make the beds or clear away the breakfast things?'

'Beds are already done, boys will do breakfast things when they get home. I've got work to do,' he turned and returned to the smithy.

'How long will Rhoda be away, John?' Mrs Titcombe asked of the farmer's back.

'Didn't say, a day or two, maybe.' He closed the smithy door.

When young Thomas Carter returned from his duties about 10.00, he was given bread and cheese for his lunch, and was packed off to school with his brother. A casual remark to his father as to the whereabouts of his stepmother was answered by a curt 'Gone to see your aunt in Eastleech for a couple of days. Get home from school early as there is extra work to do.'

Anne Butler lived opposite her friend, Rhoda Carter, in the one street in the tiny hamlet of Watchfield. Anne, of similar age to Rhoda, had been hanging clothes in the garden, when she noticed the black, heavy smoke rising from the Carter's smithy. Worse than the smoke was the sickly stench that accompanied it.

It was now three in the afternoon, and the offensive odour had been plaguing the neighbours since 10.30 in the morning. If Anne could catch sight of Rhoda, she would say something, but she was loathe to speak to John if she could help it. He had barred Anne from the house after he had found out that the pair of them had spent an hour in the local pub after shopping one evening.

At 3.30, Anne Butler could bear it no longer. She crossed the road and hammered on the heavy smithy door.

'Go away,' was Carter's response. 'You are a loose woman and are not welcome on my property.'

'Where is Rhoda?' enquired Anne.

'Up at Eastleech, and away from your damned influence.'

Anne Butler could do no more but return home.

Thomas Carter returned from school at 4.30 and was straightaway despatched half-a-mile to the only shop for 28lb of coal. On his return he was stopped by Mrs Titcombe and questioned about his stepmother. His inability to answer her queries turned a suspicious woman into a deeply apprehensive one.

Mrs Titcombe's nagging suspicions had been aroused by several points. If Rhoda had gone to see her sister in Eastleech, surely she would have called in to see if she had any messages. Secondly there was the green coat. Carter brought her little enough, and this was one of the few exceptions. Surely she would have worn it to show off to her relatives. A cream blouse and skirt could be seen through the window. All these were Rhoda's pride and joy, and she would hardly spend two days away without them.

On 22 July, David Titcombe, Rhoda's brother, took the day off work. His mother had met Anne Butler that morning. Smoke was again billowing from the Carter's smithy. All three were suspicious and worried.

At 9.30 Titcombe knocked on the farmer's door.

'What on earth are you doing, John? You'll have the house on fire.' Carter opened the door a couple of inches.

'Hello, Dave,' he said, 'I was just boiling up some water for a shave.'

'For a shave? For a shave, John? You could shave the whole damn British army in that bloody great cauldron of water.'

Dave Titcombe pushed his way into the room.

'Well I was thinking of boiling up some offal afterwards.'

'Is that what you were doing yesterday? You stank the whole village out. I shouldn't do it again today or they'll have the law on you. Let me help you put it out.'

The two men poured water on the fire and then Carter's brother-in-law left.

But Dave Titcombe was not satisfied. In fact he was far from satisfied. When he returned to the two worried women, decisions were made. Anne Butler was dispatched to collect a policeman, and Dave Titcombe went to Eastleech to see if his sister had arrived.

PC Sparkes balanced his robust figure upon his bicycle, to ride the mile to Carter's farmhouse. He was the old-fashioned type, intelligent and analytical. He knew his locals and was a fine judge of character. Carter he had known for some ten years, firstly at Shrivenham, three miles away in the Vale of the White Horse, and now at Watchfield. He found him a hard-working and honest man, if a little curt and tacit.

Rhoda he had also known for some time. He liked her, she was fun, but not entirely suited to Carter's chaste outlook. As he pedalled slowly towards the farmhouse, logic told the village constable he was on a fool's errand. Rhoda had probably gone to see her sister. Dave Titcombe was probably on his way back right now.

What was Eastleech now? Fifteen miles, thirty miles round trip, cross-country on a bike, time for a chat, say about three-and-a-half to four hours. Dave would be back at two and the worry would be over. Still, he would give Carter a call. Anne Butler's attitude was a bit alarmist. She was a good looker, if a bit flighty for these parts.

PC Sparkes lodged his bike against Carter's fence, knocked on the door and, getting no reply, he sauntered round the premises peering through each window — nothing seemed out of place or obviously suspicious.

Deciding to return later, he remounted his bike and returned to his police house.

PC Sparkes was a little more concerned when Dave Titcombe returned to say that Rhoda had not shown up at her sister's at Eastleech. He once again cycled to the Carter's farm. John Carter was still not there. The boys were with Mrs Titcombe and young Thomas reported that his father was concerned about Rhoda and had gone in search of her.

PC Sparkes made a third and successful attempt at interviewing John Carter on 23 July. The boys were at school and the farmer cordially invited him in.

The village bobby's eyes scanned the room. The place was tidy with nothing obviously amiss. As the gaunt farmer spoke, Sparkes noticed dried blood on his shirt front where it met his breeches. This in itself was easily explained. A man who deals with animals all day is certain to get a little blood about him, but it was worth making a mental note of it.

'I do not know where my wife is, I only wish I did,' Carter was replying to the constable's question. 'I spent yesterday at Eastleech, Highworth and Letchlade, searching for her, but none of her relatives could give me a clue. I do believe she has left me.'

PC Sparkes did not believe him. It was a strange sort of woman who runs off leaving her clothes behind. He knew Carter was lying, but at that precise moment he could do little except inspect the premises and then write up his notes. He thanked John Carter for his time and left.

On 25 July, John Carter walked into a Wantage pub and had a drink with his brother. 'I must confess something to you,' he said. 'I have killed my wife.' He then got up and left.

On 26 July 9am, after a night of wrestling with his conscience, Carter's brother walked into Wantage police station and announced, 'My brother, John Carter, admitted to me last night that he had killed his wife.'

Later that morning, Sergeant Benning left Wantage police station with two constables, picked up PC Sparkes, and went to arrest John Carter. Benning knew he had sufficient evidence — a missing wife, a husband who had obviously lied, and an admission of guilt, albeit by word of mouth. Now Benning wanted a thorough search and with Carter in custody this should pose no problem.

The officers knocked at the farm door, the farmer was charged, handcuffed and then returned to Wantage. Carter went quietly with a resigned look, his two young sons standing bemused and bewildered. After escorting the two boys to the Titcombes', Benning and Sparkes began their search. They went through from the house to the barn, from the barn to the smithy, and then finally to the stables. There, less than three inches below the surface, they found the body of Rhoda Anne Carter. It was doubled up, wearing nothing but a chemise. The nose had been smashed, the throat was terribly bruised, and there had been attempts to both burn and boil the remains.

After a month in custody, John Carter appeared at Wantage on 26 August, 1893, charged with the murder of his wife. He was remanded to await trial at Reading Assizes.

While John Carter waited in custody, local police began wondering about the strange disappearance of the farmer's second wife. The lady, according to Carter, had walked out on him some four years previously. Local villagers had been suspicious from the start, Why would a young woman, devoted to her children, walk out on a five-year-old boy and a mere baby?

Carter had told the police at the time they had a row over money and his wife had walked out, never to return.

In view of the death of Rhoda, old suspicions were aroused. Police interviewed a neighbour, Mrs Enstone, who described violent rows between the couple. She suggested that they excavate an area known as Burnt Leaze, which was a favourite walking place of Carter.

Police officers from Faringdon and Wantage spent days digging the site, but no remains were ever discovered.

John Carter was charged with the murder of his third wife, Rhoda Anne Carter, on 16 November 1893. He pleaded not guilty. Mr Justice Cave presided, for the prosecution were Messrs Darling and Daniel, and for the defence, Macarthy and Sherwood. Formidable evidence for the prosecution was provided by Sergeant Benning, PC Sparkes, Mrs Titcombe, David Titcombe, Anne Butler and even young Thomas Carter. Another witness, Carter's cousin, Miss Lucy Cox, gave evidence of his uncontrollable temper. She witnessed an incident at a dance on 7 June. Rhoda Carter had danced briefly with another man, and Carter had burst into a fit of violent temper, verging on the insane.

Mr Spackerman, a surgeon, whose unenviable task it was to ascertain the cause of death, said Rhoda met her demise due to strangulation. This was bad news for Carter.

Macarthy, the defence lawyer, found himself in the position of trying to defend the indefensible and justify the unjustifiable.

He pointed out that the prisoner did not deny that he had killed his wife, but it was a spur-of-the-moment loss of temper, and that his client had panicked and tried to conceal the body. He told the jury that the crime was motiveless and in no way premeditated. Carter had not meant to kill his wife, and the intention was only to strike her; the terrible and unfortunate consequences were not of his design. The charge against Carter should be one of manslaughter.

Unfortunately for Carter, Spackerman's evidence of an assault followed by strangulation seemed a complete contradiction of Macarthy's opinion.

Mr Justice Cave, in his summing up, went to some lengths to inform the jury that, even when the taking of a human life appears on the surface a motiveless crime, this does not automatically make it manslaughter. Carter was charged with murder. They must now retire and decide whether he was guilty or not guilty of the charge.

The jury did retire, for several minutes, before returning a verdict of guilty as charged. John Carter was sentenced to death and hanged at Reading Gaol on 3 December 1893.

Of the strange and disturbing disappearance of Carter's second wife, nothing more was heard. With no body, there could be no charge. Carter's first wife died of a strange accident on the farm where they both worked. Not a lucky man with wives, John Carter.

WANTAGE MARKET SQUARE — HERE CARTER CONFESSED TO HIS BROTHER.

WATCHFIELD IS ON THE EXTREME LEFT EDGE IN THIS 1864 POST OFFICE MAP OF BERKSHIRE. (CB)

PC JOSEPH CHARLTON — VICTIM OF A PUB AFFRAY.

CHARLTON'S ASSAILANTS IN CUSTODY — SLATTER AND JAMES.

MANSLAUGHTER AT HARWELL

It was Eastertide in the small Berkshire village of Harwell, the date was 3 April 1899, and it was a public holiday.

At 7.30 in the evening, the local inn, the Chequers, was doing a roaring trade. The customers were mostly farming folk, a hard-working and hard-drinking set of locals who,in general, were convivial and congenial. Isaac Day, however, was slightly apprehensive. He had been landlord of the village inn for a number of years and had developed the publicans' inborn instinct for recognising potential trouble. His concern was heightened when he saw a local trouble-maker, a man called Slatter.

Joseph Slatter was a local vagrant who travelled the vicinity, sleeping rough, and doing odd jobs. He supplemented his income by poaching, gambling and out-and-out thieving. He was well-known for his unsolicited and gratuitous violence. Slatter was trouble and Isaac Day did not want his company. In fact he had barred him some three weeks previously in mid-March. The landlord had not noticed him come in, or he would have refused to serve him. Slatter had probably slipped in with the crowd and been served by his wife while he was grabbing a swift meal in the kitchen.

Day noticed that Slatter was accompanied by a younger man, much of the same ilk. He knew the local man to be in his mid-forties, and he adjudged his companion a little over 30. The two were already beginning to create an atmosphere. Their conversations with the locals was verging on the insulting, and they had, on several occasions, picked up and quaffed other men's beer, by design, but feigning error.

Day decided things were about to get out of hand, so he despatched his pot-boy to fetch PC Hewett, the village constable.

Thomas Hewett was off duty and having a quiet glass of stout and a chinwag on his front doorstep. John Charlton, another constable from neighbouring East Hendred, was enjoying his company whe the landlord's pot-boy approached them, informing them that his guv'nor was a bit uneasy about his situation.

'Old Joe Slatter playing up again, is he?' said Hewett as he reached for his jacket. 'Tell Isaac I'll be down in a minute.'

As the young boy sped off to reassure his worried employer, the two constables walked the few hundred yards from the police house to the Chequers.

In the short time it had taken to procure the services of the constabulary, the situation had steadily worsened at the Harwell inn. Slatter and his friend, Robert James, had run out of ready cash and had resorted to begging with menaces from the more vulnerable customers. Slatter was standing over a youth and his girlfriend in the corner. James was at his side.

'Lend us a few pence for a pint, mate. You are a pretty boy, isn't he a pretty boy, Bob? Stay pretty, there's a good boy. I bet your young girl likes pretty boys. Just a penny or two to get my mate Bob and me a drink.' There was more than a hint of imminent violence in every word, and thinly veiled intimidation in every syllable.

Isaac Day had had enough. A large and robust man, he strode across the floor and stood firmly in front of Slatter. 'I've barred you before, Joe. You've crept back unbeknown to me. Now kindly get out and stop annoying my customers.'

'I ain't breaking no law, guvnor, I'm just borrowing a few pence off my friend here for a drink.' Slatter indicated the youngster he had approached.

'You are begging, Joe, and begging is against the law in this country. Now finish your ale and be off.'

'Now my mate Bob here, is a singer, lovely singer is Bob. If he was to sing to you guvnor, and then we had a little collection, now that wouldn't be begging now would it?'

The situation was rapidly heading towards the ultimate confrontation in which neither side could back down.

At this moment the door opened and Constables Hewett and Charlton entered. The situation was momentarily defused. The landlord joined the officers in the bar parlour, while Slatter brusquely shrugged his shoulders and indulged in muted conversation with James.

The constables were poured a drink by Day. They decided that a low profile was the best way to redeem the situation and restore order. Hewett felt their mere presence would calm matters down.

Unfortunately there is an exception to every rule. It was only a matter of minutes before they heard an eruption in the tap room. There was no doubt that Slatter and James were involved. Hewett despatched Charlton around the outside of the inn to meet them at the outside door, while he and the landlord hurried through to the tap room.

Hewett decided on swift and immediate action. Beer had been thrown over a local and Slatter was obviously to blame. The young constable and the landlord each grabbed a combatant and frogmarched them into the village street. There the melée continued. Slatter and James, casting off their jackets, stood there with clenched fists. 'Fight you cowardly bastards,' they yelled, 'man to man, you yellow sods.'

PC Thomas Hewett turned to follow the landlord back into the public house. He was not a man to be taunted into action; his function was to eject troublemakers. This he had done; his duty was complete.

It was at that precise moment that James became aware of PC Charlton. The young constable had come round the side of the inn, ready to support Hewett. James flew at the officer, catching him by surprise. The vagrant headbutted him, driving him to the ground. John Charlton fell heavily, cracking his skull on a kerbstone. He lay there motionless, while James and Slatter kicked him.

Hewett turned and rushed to help his comrade. He grappled with Slatter, tearing him away from the motionless body. The constable struck Slatter on the face, downing him. He was then attacked by James, but gave him the same treatment. A pitched battle followed between the constable and his two protagonists, an engagement that was to last for ten to twelve minutes, an exceptionally long time for an affray. They were joined by a growing audience who left the pub to watch the spectacle, jeering and shouting and offering encouragement.

Inevitably, as the affray continued, PC Thomas Hewett began to get the worst of it. Young and strong as a bull as he was, the superior odds were beginning to tell. Twice he had fallen.

Then Hewett noticed James Bosley, the local coalmerchant, in the crowd. 'For God's sake, Jimmy, get my stick and cuffs from the bar.'

Bosley disappeared, returning with Isaac Day and Thomas Hughes, the local butcher. Together they pushed their way through the onlookers and supplied the bloodsoaked constable with his truncheon and handcuffs.

The assistance, however late in the day, gave Hewett a new lease of life; he flew at Slatter, striking him so hard with his police stick that he split it in pieces and knocked him out. Bosley and Hughes knelt on him and manacled his hands behind his back. Hewett, blood pouring from his face, looked for James, but he was gone. Robert James had taken to the hills.

PC Thomas Hewett's first comprehensible thoughts were for his colleague. John Charlton had not moved since the first encounter. While Mrs Day attempted to stem the blood flowing from his battered face, he strode across the courtyard to where his comrade lay, now surrounded by interested bystanders. Charlton was picked up and carried to Hewett's house where medical help was soon to hand.

At 5am on Tuesday 4 April 1899, PC John Charlton, popular village constable, loving husband and father of four young children, passed away without regaining consciousness.

Much of the population of the village crowded into PC Hewett's police house for the official inquest. It was held the following day before Mr Bromley Challenor of Abingdon. Many witnesses were called who gave virtually word-for-word accounts of the happenings at the Chequers.

Mr Rice, a surgeon, stated that PC Charlton had died from pressure to the brain caused by a fracture of the skull, this in turn being consistent with the young constable's head hitting the kerb during the affray.

Much evidence was contributed by PC Hewett who seemed badly shaken. He had temporarily lost the sight of one eye, the other was badly disfigured, his nose was broken and there was severe bruising to nearly fifty percent of the officer's body.

The coroner brought in a verdict of wilful murder. He then turned on the assembled crowd and mounted a scathing verbal attack on them. Bromley Challener said that he found it inconceivable, nay incomprehensible that so many local people could stand by and watch two courageous policemen set upon by rogues, and do nothing while these same officers received such grievous wounds that one had since died and the other would be incapacitated for months to come. The coroner closed the court, and the villagers filtered from the room.

Joseph Slatter made a brief and taciturn appearance at Wantage Petty Sessions before Mr H. D. de Vitre. He was unforthcoming to say the least. New evidence came in. Mr Brain, for the prosecution, brought forward several witnesses who stated under oath that they had heard Slatter encourage James to stab PC Hewett with a sheath knife. Bosley, Hughes and the landlord, Isaac Day, stated on oath that they had heard Slatter screaming repeatedly, 'Stick the ——— with your chiv, Bob.' It must be said on James's behalf that he refrained from doing so.

After this concise and succinct evidence, de Vitre thought it prudent to adjourn to Berkshire Assizes. Joseph Slatter was remanded in police custody.

Robert James *alias* Smith had last been seen at 5 o'clock on Tuesday 4 April, crossing the Thames at Streatley Bridge into Oxfordshire. He had obviously travelled the ten miles from Harwell overnight. Superintendent Davis from Reading was put on his trail. He despatched various officers to villages north of the Thames, and local PCs kept an eye on the sparse river crossings in case James should double back into Berkshire. Davis wired his colleagues at Oxford. He described James as of medium height, aged about thirty, dark, with a moustache, and wearing a scruffy frock coat and bowler hat.

Reports were soon coming in of a man of that description heading towards the Chilterns. He had been sighted at Woodcote and again with the gypsies at the village of Checkendon. Tracing a line in a north-easterly direction, that followed the path that James had already taken towards the Chilterns where he was known to have relatives, the police were able to predict that James would surface in either Ipsden or Stoke Row, two tiny neighbouring hamlets.

PC John Timms, the local constable, was contacted and told to be on the look-out. Within a few minutes he had noticed a scruffy individual walk into the Oak public house, Stoke Row.

The arrest was a quiet, almost casual affair. PC Timms strolled into the inn, confronted the man at the bar and accused him of being Robert James, wanted for the murder of a police officer at Harwell.

James came quietly. He was visibly shaken and seemed genuinely surprised that Charlton was dead. He repeatedly stated to Timms, 'It was a fair fight, two onto two, I'm sorry, I didn't know the man had died.'

Robert James, *alias* Smith, was locked in Reading Gaol overnight and then escorted to Wantage the following morning. He had been on the run a mere two days.

At the Berkshire Assizes on 16 June, Joseph Slatter, 46, and Robert James, 31, appeared before Justice Day. Under his recommendation, the charge was reduced to manslaughter. Both pleaded not guilty.

Messrs Nash and Mordaunt Snagge for the prosecution were eloquent and scathing. Numerous witnesses for the prosecution followed each other with almost boring repetition into the box. Each took the oath and then gave almost identical evidence, one after the other condemning the prisoners in the dock.

Slatter stood nonchalantly. He was no stranger to justice. He heard himself described as an undesirable scourge of the neighbourhood by several witnesses. He stood taut, arrogant and oblivious to the seriousness of his situation.

James, on the other hand, had plenty to say. He had been drinking all day with Slatter on 3 April, they had consumed some fourteen or fifteen quarts of ale, they had entered the Chequers, where they had been involved in an argument with two large men he now knew to be Hewett and Charlton. He had not known at the time that they were officers of the law. They were in plain clothes and, in his opinion, drunk, arrogant and overpowering. The fight that ensued was a fair fight and he had no idea until he was arrested at Stoke Row that the unfortunate man had died. He was sorry about the outcome of an affray that he had not started and in no way wanted.

Much of James's statement had more than a modicum of truth. Several witnesses said that Slatter started the brawl. However, it was obviously a blatant lie that he had no idea that Hewett and Charlton were police officers. When the constable first entered the Chequers, albeit in plain clothes, Slatter, the local man, had obviously left James in no doubt who they were. Having seen through this, the jury treated the remainder of James's evidence with scepticism.

After a rather unnecessarily long and elaborate trial, Justice Day's summing-up was refreshingly brief. He pointed out that a young officer's life had been tragically taken while doing his duty, protecting others. If, in the jury's opinion, the prosecution had proved beyond all doubt that the two men in the dock were responsible for this brave young constable's demise, then they had but one course, and that was to bring a verdict of guilty of manslaughter.

The verdict was not long in coming. The jury returned within minutes, finding both men guilty. Justice Day sentenced them both to 20 years' penal servitude. Without a word, both men left the dock.

A massive collection was made for Charlton's young widow and four children. The untimely death of his father did nothing to alter the youngest Charlton's ambition. He joined the Reading Police and served with distinction for a number of years.

THE CHEQUERS AT HARWELL.

JAMES CROSSED THE THAMES AT STREATLEY. (CB)

EAST HENDRED — PC CHARLTON'S BEAT: CHAPEL SQUARE APPROPRIATELY BOASTED A PILLORY AND GALLOWS. (VDMC)

AMY ROBSART AND THE EARL OF LEICESTER. (MC)

The Spirit of Cumnor

Little remains of the once awsomely splendid Cumnor Place, home of Robert Dudley and Amy Robsart. All that exists of the imposing dwelling is a few feet of wall and an open fireplace adjoining Cumnor Church.

There are, however, remnants of the unexplained mystery that rocked the developed world of 1560. In the church vestry can be found the unsmiling and stalwart statue of Queen Elizabeth I. This eminent likeness of the sovereign was commissioned by Dudley to adorn and embellish the gardens of Cumnor. There is also a collection of copies of Dudley's and Amy's letters and a portrait of this beautiful young woman. There are bills from London tailors and hat-makers and the same building holds the tomb of Anthony Foster, thought by many to be instrumental in the demise of this popular young woman.

Eight years after her marriage to Robert Dudley, Amy Robsart, daughter of a Norfolk knighted gentleman, moved from Lincolnshire to Berkshire to take up the vast abode that her charming if rakish husband had provided for her.

Amy was immensely happy. In her eyes the marriage was good, life with Robert was still exciting, he was ambitious and popular at court, and he also kept her in a high degree of affluence.

The couple stayed briefly with friends of Robert's, the Hydes of Denchworth, before moving into Dumnor Place. Here Amy was introduced to Dudley's steward, household manager and personal friend, Anthony Foster.

Rumours were beginning to circulate at the time, concerning Robert Dudley and Her Sovereign Majesty, Elizabeth I. It was true Dudley spent most of his time at court and it was also true that he was one of the Queen's favourites, but surely such was the path to wealth and advancement.

Amy ignored the rumours as tittle-tattle and gossip. She was more than happy to busy herself with her new home. Anthony Foster was a Godsend in this respect. Disregarding his work as Member of Parliament for Abingdon almost to the point of neglect, he helped Amy with every decision and chore.

On Sunday 8 September 1560, a mop fair was held at nearby Abingdon. As a treat for her large staff, who had been so assiduous over the period of moving in, Amy encouraged them to go. (It was suggested later that she had insisted they go.) She assured her staff that she would be quite safe chatting with three of her lady friends.

The staff left with instructions not to hurry back.

Two of Amy's friends returned to their respective homes about 6pm, and the third, a Mrs Owen, dined with the attractive young mistress and left about 9pm. Amy assured the concerned woman that she would be alright and the staff would be returning about 11pm.

At 11.30pm a band of jubilant household staff returned to Cumnor Hall from the mop fair. They were surprised to find the house in total darkness. They at once set about lighting candles and lanterns and almost immediately found the body of their beautiful young mistress at the bottom of the main staircase.

Her neck had been broken, there was bruising around the throat that suggested strangulation and blue-black bruising around the lips, that suggested poison had been forced between them. To the old question, did she fall, or was she pushed? were added two more refinements: was she also choked or poisoned?

Dudley was officially to hear of his wife's death the following day, when a messenger was despatched from Cumnor Place to Windsor Castle where he was with the Queen.

Dudley's reaction was enigmatic, his actions unfathomable. The devoted husband did not himself go to Cumnor, but sent his cousin, Sir Thomas Blount, to investigate. Also, he had Amy's body sent down to Worcester College, Oxford, where it was interned with costly pageantry and ostentation. The expenses were immense for Elizabethan times, and yet, strangely enough, despite all the pomp and lavish grandeur, Dudley kept well away from the funeral.

Rumour was rife the length and breadth of Europe. Dudley had plotted with Elizabeth. They had sent a message to the country stating that Amy was ill, shortly before her death. At this time and prior to the fatal evening, Amy Robsart had enjoyed the most robust of health. There was little, if any, evidence to substantiate the gossip and, by the same token, there was little to disprove it.

It did, however, come to light some seven years later that a Dr Bayley, a professor at Oxford, had been approached by one of Dudley's servants shortly before Amy's death. This servant had asked for a physic as his mistress was unwell. Bayley, knowing this not to be the case, suspecting foul play and fearing for his own safety, refused to supply one.

Sir Thomas Blount's half-hearted investigation into Amy's death was absolutely barren. He was, when all is said and done, Dudley's man. It is unlikely that he investigated too deeply for fear of aggravating and embarrassing his master. Blount met with a convenient wall of silence.

There was persistent rumour (probably close to the truth) bandied about by the local gentry, that Anthony Foster had hidden himself with a paid labourer at Cumnor Place. After waiting for Amy's company to leave, they had tried to force poison down the young woman's throat. Failing in this they had then strangled her and thrown the body downstairs to give the appearance of suicide.

What seemed to support this theory was that Anthony Foster was said to have been strangled shortly afterwards, thereby tying up all the loose ends and avoiding embarrassment in the future.

At the subsequent hearing all records from the coroner's office pertaining to cause of death were conveniently mislaid. It was also noted that both Blount and Dudley had approached the jury with nauseating regularity prior to the enquiry. It is thought that many of the jury became wealthy men, through bribes by both Blount and Dudley, so that they arrived at the same conclusion — a conclusion that 'After a searching enquiry, they could find no presumption of evil doing.' The case was dropped. Of Amy Robsart's death, there is little else to report.

After the enquiry, Dudley drew closer to the Queen. His wife's demise was convenient; an obstruction fortuitously swept away.

Dudley acquired much power in the kingdom, but he never married the Queen. Instead, he secretly married the daughter of Lord Howard of Effingham. When Elizabeth discovered this clandestine liaison, she was livid and when, some short time later, it was discovered that Dudley found his second wife an inconvenience and tried to poison her, the whole Amy Robsart affair flared up once more. Dudley's many enemies at court tried to renew the charge of murder, yet Robert Dudley escaped. His still close, but strained relationship with his sovereign made him virtually invulnerable.

Being a man who enjoyed life on the cutting edge, Dudley then indulged in a bigamous and secretive third marriage to Lettice Knollys. On hearing this the Queen's anger knewno bounds. She summoned him to court, chastised him ferociously and slapped his face before the entire assembly. She then swore that she would throw Dudley and his she-wolf into the tower.

Robert Dudley left with haste, realising that he had gone too far this time, and it seemed doubtful his beloved monarch would ever forgive him. Dudley tried to sink into obscurity. He no doubt found this preferable to spending the remainder of his days in the Tower.

Dudley spent some seven years of obscurity until Elizabeth I once again forgve him, when in 1585 she decided to support the Dutch against the Spanish, and placed Dudley in command. His uninspired and inglorious career is chiefly remembered for his unsuccessful siege of Zutphen in which his own nephew, Sir Philip Sidney, was killed.

Dudley was recalled in 1587, and, despite his abysmal failures, was held in high esteem at court once again. In 1588, Robert Dudley's health was not good. He was 56 years old and was heading for his magnificent home in Warwickshire, Kenilworth Castle. On his way he visited Rycote House in Oxfordshire to write a letter to his beloved monarch. He then proceeded to another of his homes, Cornbury Park, where he relaxed and took in a little hunting.

It is reported that, while out riding in Wychwood Forest, he suddenly came face to face with the shade of Amy Robsart. He returned to Cornbury a broken and terrified man. There he died five days later.

It is doubtful that Amy Robsart's spirit appeared at Cornbury to hasten Dudley's end. If it did seek revenge, the lady's spirit certainly took its time. It was some 28 years between the death of Amy Robsart and the death of Robert Dudley.

There is much more evidence of Amy's spirit at Cumnor. Shortly after her death, terrifying screams were heard from the staircase where she died.

Tenants came and went with great rapidity. No-one stayed longer than a few weeks. All complained of shreiks from the area at the bottom of the stairs. Dudley never stayed another night within the building.

The ominous old house stayed empty for years. Then there was an attempt to exorcise poor Amy's unquiet spirit. Nine priests came down from Oxford and tried to lay the troubled soul to rest in a nearby pool. That place was afterwards known as Lady Dudley's Pond. Apparently this did nothing to alleviate the situation, and the house was uninhabited for many further years and then fell into disrepair.

In 1814, Cumnor Place was deemed no longer habitable and was demolished, many of the stones appropriated by the Earl of Abingdon to rebuild Wytham Church.

As recently as the 1980s screams have been heard near the church at Cumnor. They seem to rise in a brief but sometimes piercing crescendo from the area of the stairwell at Cumnor Place.

CUMNOR PLACE WAS HOME TO DUDLEY, AND TO AMY ROBSART. (MC)

THE RIVERBANK AT ABINGDON WAS WHERE THE MOP FAIR WAS HELD — THE DAY THAT AMY DIED. (CB)

JOHN HUTT'S VILLAGE — BRAY EARLY THIS CENTURY. (CB)

THE END OF THE ROAD FOR HUTT — READING, HERE IN 1823. (CB)

TRAGEDY AT TOUCHEN END

Touchen End is a small hamlet that straddles the Bracknell to Maidenhead road. Today it consists of a pub, several market gardens and a string of houses. The population is sparse. This in itself is unusual for East Berkshire where every conceivable back yard, nook and cranny has obtained building permission. Touchen End has, as yet, escaped the sprawl of development.

In 1800 there was a baker's shop in Touchen End. Its proprietor was Thomas Pearman. Thomas was a popular man of about thirty-five, and happily married to Anne, an attractive woman some five years his junior. The couple had taken over the shop six years previously and had achieved a healthy profit through hard work. They had also produced a daughter, a spritely mite, five years old.

Wednesday 12 February 1800 was a commonplace day as far as the Pearmans were concerned. The organisation and roster of labour was much the same as usual. Thomas arose at 3am, for the hours of a baker are notoriously unsocial, he prepared the dough and moulds and began baking. Ann would join her jusband at 5.30am and then the pair would work diligently together until 7am when Ann would cook breakfast and awaken their daughter. At 9am the small shop would open, Ann would serve at the counter, and Thomas would deliver loaves to their immediate neighbours on foot.

Thus Wednesday 12 February went much the usual affable way. The small family lunched together and then at 2pm Thomas hitched the pony to his small cart and set off to make deliveries to farms and cottages in the more remote areas of nearby Winkfield Plain.

Some fifteen minutes after Thomas departed, accompanied by his small daughter, two elderly ladies were heading for the bakery to buy some salt. As they neared the small shop they were nearly knocked to the ground by a young man fleeing from the same direction. Both ladies were to say later that they knew the young man by sight, but not by name.

At the bakery the ladies were surprised to find the shop had not been opened after Ann Pearman's brief lunchbreak. It was now 2.20. They waited several minutes and then went to the back of the building where the family's living quarters were. They knocked on the door and, when there was no answer, they became concerned. Concern accelerated to alarm when one of the ladies heard alow moaning from the family's kitchen.

One stayed behind and the other hurried as fast as her advancing years would permit, to fetch a neighbour from a nearby cottage. The man listened intently at the Pearman's door for some seconds before he too heard the low and feeble moan from the kitchen. When he was sure it was not part of geriatric panic or imagination, he went quickly to the Pearman's stable, found a crowbar, and levered the cottage door open.

Nothing in the three villagers' long but sheltered past could have prepared them for the horrendous sight that met their eyes.

At 2pm on Wednesday 12 February, John Hutt sat in a dry ditch within easy view of the small Touchen End baker's shop. He had been there about forty minutes watching the comings and goings of the little business. John had taken a faggot from the pile outside the shop and, while he waited for Thomas Pearman to depart on his regular afternoon round, he had cut and whittled the faggot into an easily manageable cudgel. Later, at his trial, when the many chippings were exhibited, John's fate was sealed. The prosecution laboured long on the amount of time the whittling had taken which therefore proved considerable premeditation.

John Hutt was a youth of 19 from a poor but upright Christian family. He was experiencing the limited pleasures and drawbacks of early manhood. Hutt was small, 5′2″, and did his best to compensate for this by attempting to achieve status as a local spender, a pretence at affluence his lowly job as a labourer did not support.

John Hutt was in debt, not to any great extent, but enough to be embarrassing. He had decided to remedy this inconvenience by robbing Pearman's bakery. His plan was to wait until Pearman had left, and then creep up on the baker's young wife, knock her unconscious with the cudgel, and be off with the takings.

Just after 2pm he made his way to the back door. It was ajar and he could see the young woman busying herself with chores before reopening the shop for the afternoon trade. Hutt crept silently into the kitchen, his hands sweating profusely as he closed in on his prey. He stood less than a yard from his victim, but she did not look up. Hutt struck her from behind with some force, expecting the young woman to go down. She merely swayed and turned towards him, a look of horror and disbelief crossing her attractive young features. He struck again with all his might. The young woman stumbled. Hutt panicked and struck again and again and again until his defenceless victim fell to the floor.

Blind panic now ruled him; he raced through the connecting door into the shop, ransacked the till and then hurriedly retreated through the back door, locking it and throwing the key into the ditch.

John Hutt fled down the small village main street, narrowly missing two elderly ladies.

The shock for the three neighbours on the discovery of Ann Pearman can well be imagined. The young woman lay across the floor of her spotless kitchen, her skull smashed with such force that the brain was exposed. The extreme force of the blows had splashed blood on the walls and ceilings. Unbelievably, the woman was still alive, but barely so.

From the nearby inn, a pot-boy was despatched to fetch a doctor from the neighbouring village of Bray, and another was sent to find a constable.

Both arrived poste-haste, but there was little the doctor could do. Ann Pearman was carried to her bedroom, where she died at 8pm.

The constable was soon joined by his colleagues and between them they obtained detailed descriptions of the man who had dashed from the direction of the bakery.

Witnesses described the running man as about 5′, of stocky build, and with an extremely florid complexion. Added to this was a distinctive mop of white hair verging on albino. There were not many people like that in a sparsely populated area where everybody knows everybody else. John Hutt's name was quickly mentioned.

The constables were speedily despatched to his home at Bray. When he had not returned by 1am, it was assumed that he was the wanted man.

Bills were posted, and added to the description was a description of the fugitive's attire: 'Breeches, short frock [coat] and yellow waistcoat.'

White haired and florid, dumpy John Hutt was on the run. The murder was on the 12th, the 13th found him in Farnham, the 15th in Petersfield, and on the 17th the fugutive was in Portsmouth, trying desperately to join the Marines. The 18th found him in the custody of two Maidenhead cavalry officers who took him back to Reading.

John Hutt was tried on 4 March 1800. He took a surly, sullen and arrogant attitude while giving his evidence. He denied that he had committed such a horrendous action, and claimed to be the victim of circumstances.

The evidence, both factual and circumstantial, weighed heavily against the young man. After a six hour trial, the jury retired for a further two hours before bringing a verdict of guilty.

The law in 1800 made no provision for any other sentence but death, there was no appeal procedure, and the law stipulated that the prisoner should be executed within 48 hours of being found guilty; John Hutt's termination was scheduled for 6 March. Also, as was usual in 1800, the judge directed that the corpse be publicly dissected at Reading Town Hall.

Shortly before his execution, John Hutt admitted the murder of Ann Pearman.

COMBE GIBBET.

BERKSHIRE MURDERS IN BRIEF

In 1661, George Staverton, a wealthy but reportedly hen-pecked businessman of Wokingham, bequesthed the princely sum of £6 per annum to provide a bull to be baited yearly. The event was to take place on 21 December, St Thomas's Day. The bequest financed bullbaiting for 162 years, until it was outlawed in 1823.

Bullbaiting was a cruel exhibition wherein the tortured and eventually demented animal was chased through the streets by specially trained dogs and gleefully cheering citizens. Then, when it finally dropped from exhaustion, it was killed.

It was a spectator sport where young men would show their courage by standing in the path of the maddened bull and then leaping side at the last moment.

Crowd violence did not arrive with the football hooligans. A report in the 18th century states that, at the annual bullbaiting, 'A body of roughs known as the Wokingham Fighters was notorious. They would pick quarrels, especially with strangers, and the fights would take place at the Cockpit, often witnessed by members of the council.'

During the bullbaiting, thousands tore through the narrow streets of Wokingham, providing a splendid opportunity for the disaffected and unscrupulous to push their unwanted spouses or other associates in the path of the stampede. Such actions were virtually undetectable, and on several occasions suspicion there might be, but proof was impossible.

A report in 1794 states, 'Elizabeth North was buried on December 26th 1794. She was found dead, terribly bruised, the morning after bullbaiting. The Coroner, with his inquest, found her ''accidentally dead''.' There is also a side note: 'A man taken from the bull is without hope of life.' Another unfortunate victim was Martha May, who died after being hurt by Wokingham Fighters' bullbaiting in 1808.

There is no record of how many people lost their lives, either accidentally or otherwise, but nobody was ever charged with an offence.

It is also impossible to ascertain the outcome of another Wokingham murder. The 1797 church chronicles lament the demise of one Edward Bunce, a gatekeeper at Coppid Beech Lane turnpike, who was found murdered in the night.

In 1854 a young servant girl aged 22, Louisa Parsons, attended a party at Playhatch, some two miles north-east of Caversham. Louisa, an attractive girl full of life was in service at Mapledurham. The party was a lively affair, with the young girl surrounded by people of her own age. Unfortunately, partway through the festivities, Louisa was taken ill with severe pains in her stomach. She was taken home, where her conditon worsened.

Louisa's parents were country folk and believed very much in herbal remedies. The regular doctor was called, but he was forced to work in conjunction with 'Grannie Patin', a self-appointed cure-all from Mapledurham.

Neither the accepted medical help, nor the quackery were of much use, for poor Louisa died early the following morning. There is no record that an autopsy was carried out.

Louisa's parents decided that their daughter had been murdered. They suspected she had been poisoned at the party. The police were called but nobody was ever charged. There was considerable debate as to whether any crime had been committed after all.

Her parents remained adamant, so much so that they consulted Granny Patin concerning the wording on their daughter's tombstone. The outcome was: 'Sacred to the memory of Louisa, daughter of George and Mary Parsons, died April 1854, aged 22 years. All you young people as you pass by Pray on my grave now cast an eye Beware of false lovers and their friends I died from poison you may depend.'

The mention of the word poison and the clear inference gave rise to considerable criticism in the little village. Local people found the epitaph unseemly and ostracised the Parsons.

Things came to a head when a Doctor Hawtry became Rector of Mapledurham. He found the wording offensive enough, but when he was later informed that the composition was that of a witch his anger boiled over. There followed as always, an uneasy compromise; some of the more offensive wording was covered up. But Louisa's 'murderer' was never discovered.

An ill-defined report of a possible murder comes out of the small racing town of Lambourn.

Old Lambourn Place was home to the Hippisley family for many generations. The house was originally 15th century, but it was demolished in Victorian times and the present house erected. The last of the Hippisley clan, the notorious Henry Hippisley, died there about 1890.

In the late 1880s, Henry was not a particularly popular man with local townsfolk. Bullying and overpowering, he believed that might was right and woe betide anyone who stood in his way. Feared as he was, the townsfolk had gathered to oppose him on several occasions, once when he affronted their God-fearing attitudes by ordering his men to rip the timber fan-faulting from the local church to use in the construction of Lambourn Palace. No legal action was taken so the locals were left to seethe with no redress.

On the second occasion, Henry was prosecuted. This time he had upset the might of the Charity Commissioners by defrauding them of money from local almshouses. A rather inept fine resulted.

Personifying, as he did, the local, all-powerful gentry of the day, Henry was wont to indulge in the occasional deflowering of local maidens, and it was strongly rumoured that a serving girl at Lambourn Palace had been killed by Hippisley in a fit of temper.

Fortunately for Hippisley, the body was never found, although vast areas of nearby Lambourn Woods were excavated by the townsfolk. No body, no charge — even if there was no serving girl!

If there ever was a body, Henry Hippisley took the secret to his grave — oblivious of the rumour and revilement that surrounded him in his final years — and fortunately for him, died of natural causes.

Down a gravel track near Reading's Coley Park, there is a picturesque stone bridge crossing the town's third river, the Holybrook. Not far away, silhouetting the pleasant pastures, is an ornate dovecote with other attractive buildings. All the land thereabouts, including the Great Coley Mansion, was once in the possession of the powerful Vachel family. Their ancestry can be traced in the Reading area as far back as 1240.

It was early in the 14th century when John Vachel disputed the rights across this land with the Abbot of Reading Abbey. The monks looked upon the small bridge and pathway as a God-given right of access. Vachel certainly did not.

The infuriated Abbot put forward a test case by sending a monk with a wagonload of corn across the bridge. Vachel, to prove his point, put the monk to the sword, killing him instantly; then he tipped the cart, complete with contents,into the stream below.

The Abbot's reaction was to ex-communicate him, and then fine him heavily before he could regain absolution.

Not too drastic a sentence, one might think, as peasants were hanged for stealing a loaf of bread, but as further penance, Vachel was forced to change his family motto to 'Tis better to suffer than to revenge'.

The *Reading Mercury* was founded in 1723 and one of its initial duties was to report the untimely death of a popular local farmer, Jonathon Blagrave.

It was a Saturday night in February, and Jonathon Blagrave had done well at the town's market. He was a contented man for he had a good wife, a prosperous farm in Upper Caversham some fourmiles from Reading market, had had a good season and a financially successful day. He was now returning home to Blagrave Farm.

Jon was in early middle-age. Stocky and friendly, he had two small flaws in his character which were to be his undoing. He imbibed too much, too often and too frequently and, when in his cups, was included to brag and boast. An acre became a field, a hundredweight a ton, and a guinea became a fortune.

Jonathon Blagrave had inflicted his extrovert and yet popular company on several of Reading's alehouses that evening, before crossing Caversham Bridge on his journey home. He pulled his plodding horse to a halt outside the Griffin, still a popular pub on the Oxfordshire side of the Thames. There, with several farmers of his ilk, he quaffed pint after pint of good Berkshire ale.

Jonathon knew he had less than two miles to go and that his faithful horse would trudge him home as he had done many times before. As ale and songs flowed and inhibitions retreated, Farmer Blagrave's boasting increased, the price he received for his corn became more exaggerated and an appreciative audience egged him on. He slapped his jingling pocket. 'Nobody makes profit like Jonathan Blagrave,' he shouted.

Unnoticed in the corridors of that crowded and swarming inn sat three young people — two young men and an attractive young woman. All were down on their luck, all had been drinking and all had decided on an easy way out.

Blagrave left the Griffin at about 3am on the Sunday morning. He followed the main road for a few hundred yards up St Peter's Hill and then took a track between the main road and the Thames, directly towards Blagrave Farm.

It was but a few yards across the first field that he was attacked by three footpads. His skull was smashed, but he managed to drag himself to the Roebuck (no longer there), where he later died.

The *Mercury* stated shortly afterwards that 'Three persons were took up on suspicion' and later that 'Ambrose Strange, who killed him, was hanged in chains on Tyler's Heath for it.'

There is no mention of the other two people involved or whether or not they were convicted, an Tyler's Heath is also an enigma, as there is no record of any such place in this part of Reading. It is more in keeping with Tilehurst, the other side of the Thames.

Yet there is an interesting side to the story that emerged in 1888, some 165 years later, when workmen digging in Woodcote Road, close to the murder site, discovered three bodies — of two men and a woman. The bodies had been stretched, which was consistent with being hung in chains. Woodcote Lane for centuries was part of the main Wallingford Road.

In the 18th century, examples were always set where they would have the greatest effect on the most travellers. There can be little doubt these were the remains of the gregarious farmer's ferocious assailants.

The tiny village of Combe, overshadowed by the vast and towering Inkpen Beacon, has a chilling tale to tell. Various versions have been related by the locals of this close-knit and defensive community. One version in the form of the film, *The Black Legend,* has popularised the story. The film is but one version of some horrifying events, and stretched poetic licence to the extreme.

Combe Gibbet (not the original) can be seen today, elevated above the sparse countryside. It is a timely reminder of when justice was swift and permanent. To visit the area on a summer's day, surrounded by picknickers, is pleasant enough, but to gaze across the four visible countries on a grey winter's afternoon is bleak beyond belief.

The most popularly accepted story, probably greatly altered since its origins some 300 years ago in 1676, concerns jealousy, greed, murder, the eternal triangle and every other human emotion that is a foreplay to disaster.

George Broomham was a farm labourer from East Woodhay, a nearby village. He was a hardworking, frugal and thrifty man who was saving to buy a small cottage from his employer. George had a wife, Martha, who was dumpy and plain. She was devoted to her husband, and also to their young son, Robert, a boy of six years.

Unfortunately for George Broomham, he became besotted with a local barmaid, a comely and attractive young widow, a lady of somewhat easy virtue called Dorothy Newman. Dorothy lived just over the hill at Inkpen, with her two young sons. George would spend early evenings lying on the hillside with her, professing his love.

Things were going well until Dorothy became impatient. She could see no future in her clandestine relationship. She began to tease him, flirting with other men at the pub while he stood there, morose and silent.

It was through deepening concern at losing his alliance with his lady love ,that George set out to rid himself of his wife. As they lay on the hillside in each other's arms, George Broomham outlined his plan to Dorothy. It was simplicity itself.

Martha brought him hot pasties every lunchtime from their cottage, to his place of work in the fields. At the top of a hill she passed a little oasis of trees that surrounded a small pool. He and Dorothy would lie in wait the following day and cudgel her to death. He would report her missing and the crime would doubtlessly be blamed on some tramp or itinerate worker.

Just as they planned, the couple set upon the unfortunate woman the following day, and beat her to death before pushing her body into the shallow pool. It was over in a matter of seconds. It was then tht they turned and saw Robert. The small boy must have followed his mother through the fields. He stood there wide eyed, not fully understanding the appalling scene.

George Broomham also stood there, riveted to the spot. He stared in disbelief as he watched Dorothy grab the boy and hold his head under the surface of the pool until he lay unmoving, like a small rag doll.

Dorothy Newman nudged her fellow conspirator back to reality, then they ran at breakneck speed to their respective homes. Unfortunately for Dorothy, young Robert was not the only unexpected wandered on the Inkpen Beacn that morning. Her two sons had watched the scene from a distance and were soon to report it to the authorities. This, coupled with the gossip that for some time surrounded the couple, soon convinced the constables they had the right people.

George Broomham was questioned, but only briefly, before he admitted the whole sordid affair. The unexpected death of his son had shattered him.

The murderers were tried at Winchester, and sentenced to hang at Inkpen, midway between the two villages. Gallows were specially erected, and used only once.

There is a sequel to this story not mentioned in any of the many accounts. It was gleaned from local inhabitants. Combe was once in Hampshire, but the source of constant bickering between the Berkshire and Hampshire authorities. After the trial of Broomham and Newman, the Hampshire people had no stomach for hanging the pair. Berkshire people, on the other hand, were less squeamish. They hanged the couple on the understanding that Combe would become part of Berkshire and remain so.

In 1857, Reading police force was under the auspices of Chief Constable Henry Peck, a man who played it strictly by the rule book.

In June, a well-to-do gentleman in a charged emotional state, ran into the Reading Police Station, where he was confronted by Chief Constable Peck. The agitated man shook with frustration as he tried to relate his story. Peck steadfastly adhered to protocol and insisted that the gentleman give his name and address.

After this timewasting procedure, George Shackel related how he and his manservant had been attacked by two labourers in Kings Meadow. He had left to fetch a constable, leaving his man stalwartly doing battle with the two thugs.

Peck got out the rule book. 'I am very sorry, but the law prevents my interference, unless your man is seriously hurt or a policeman is present as a witness.'

Shackel became indignant and said he would fetch a magistrate and complain about the Chief Constable's attitude, which he did.

Meanwhile, Shackel's unfortunate man had been done to death by his two attackers, and Peck now had a manslaugher case on his hands, a crime he might well have prevented.

Shortly after, the Watch Committee decided unanimously that Henry Peck was no longer the man they wanted for Chief Constable.

There was one hell of a to-do. Peck was a popular man, and both the force and the populace wanted him to stay, wo they registered their complaint of his dismissal by way of a petition.

The Committee was unyielding; Peck should go.

The people were adamant; Peck must stay.

The Committee relented. Henry Peck could keep his job as Chief Constable until he found another one. The job search took him seven years, and by that time he was ripe for retirement.

Most committees ignore touchy problems until they go away of their own accord. Two local men were later charged with the manslaughter of Shackel's manservant.

1896 was a busy year for murder in Berkshire. There was the terrible Amelia Dyer affair, which filled the national papers for some weeks, and there was the unfortunate Trooper Woolridge who was hanged at Reading Gaol for killing his young wife. There was also a third, and less sensational killing. Probably by far the most tragic and also least known of the trio was the killing of an unnamed baby by her mother, Jane Cox.

On 30 May 1896, an extremely pregnant young lady named Jane Cox was employed as a shop assistant by a young couple named Drake at their premises in Chain Street, Reading. Jane Cox was 21, attractive, single and hardworking in so far as her condition allowed.

At 11.30 at night, Jane went to bed in her small room above the shop. Her employer and friend, Susan Drake, sat mending below, awaiting her husband's return. Susan heard several groans from upstairs and, after receiving no reply, went upstairs to Jane's room. The sight that met the young housewife's eyes was appalling.

Jane Cox was standing there transfixed, her eyes staring in an inhuman gaze. There was blood streaming down her white nightdress and also soaking the bedcovers. Susan, believing her friend had suffered some form of miscarriage, shouted to her returning husband to fetch medical help.

Mr Drake returned almost immediately with a surgeon named Key, who lived nearby. Mr Key found little or no harm done to Jane Cox, but found the small body of her newborn child wrapped in the bedclothes. He ascertained that it had been a normal birth, but that terrible injuries had been inflicted on the poor child soon afterwards. The mouth and chin had been torn away and the jaw broken.

Jane finally spoke, a weeping voice begging forgiveness. She stated, 'I did it to stop the child crying. I did not know what to do with the child.'

The police were called. PC Hudson arrested the weeping girl straightaway, and took her to the Reading workhouse. At the post-mortem, further injuries were discovered. An attempt had been made at strangulation.

Key and Hudson gave evidence that Jane Cox had been quite rational when questioned shortly after the death of the child, a view that was contested by the Drakes. On 20 June Jane was indicted on a coroner's warrant on a charge of infanticide. She was found not guilty and discharged.

There are varying reports as to what happened to the distraught young woman. One is that the not guilty verdict was brought on the understanding that she sought medical help in a psychiatric hospital, and that poor Jane finished her days in Broadmoor.

BULLBAITING IN WOKINGHAM. (BCL)

CAVERSHAM BRIDGE LOOKED LIKE THIS WHEN BOASTFUL JONATHON BLAGRAVE CROSSED IT IN 1723.

MAPLEDURHAM, HOME OF LOUISA PARSONS. (CB)

*I*NDEX

Figures in *italics* refer to illustrations

READING MERCURY

AND

BERKS COUNTY PAPER.

ESTABLISHED 1723.

PRICE 2d. BY POST 2½d.

JBSCRIPTION:—Per Quarter, Prepaid, 2s. 9d.; if Booked, 3s.

Published every Saturday morning, at the Offices, Reading and Newbury, and other ch Offices, and very extensively and expeditiously circulated throughout Berkshire and e principal Towns and Villages in adjoining and distant Counties over a wide area. The

READING MERCURY

IS THE

COUNTY PAPER FOR BERKS,

has a *very large circulation* among the most influential families of the neighbourhood, as as the leading Agricultural and Commercial classes, in Berks, Bucks, Hants, Oxon, and s.

Subscribers

Presentation Copies

1. Berkshire County Council
2. Newbury Library
3. Reading Library
4. Wokingham Library
5. Bracknell Library
6. Windsor Library
7. Slough Library
8. Maidenhead Library

9 Roger Long
10 Clive & Carolyn Birch
11 Colonel R.O. Mells
12 Ruth White
13 Michael Brookes
14 T.M. Gilmour
15 Mr & Mrs P.J. Ayres
16 W. Benyon
17 Mrs Heather Lloyd
18 Mrs Carol Botterill
19 C.R.V. Searle
20 Jean Maxted
21 F. Leslie Asburrow
22 Jean T. Gardner
23 Sir W. Mount
24 Mrs J. Labab
25 Graham R. Murray
26 Janice Davidson
27 Cathy Davidson
28 Diana Davidson
29 Philip P. Doubleday
30 Harry & Ruth Willard
31 Janet Chown
32 Mrs Barbara Long
33–35 Jennifer T. Merralls
36 Neil Fraser Witney
37 Leslie Grout
38 R.N. McRae
39 Mr & Mrs J.A.H. Bexhell
40 Pamela Boyd
41 S. Butler & Miss A. Bell
42 H.J. Allen
43 John Shanahan
44 Gilbert Smith
45 Mrs M. Whitesmith
46 Mrs A. Donnelly
47 Anne Long
48 Stanley Stroud
49 V.J. Pocock
50 Jill Wrapson
51 Michael Abbott
52 Lt Col A.B. Clarke
53 J. Allen
54 M.T. Bell
55 Mrs Fitch
56 Mabel Wilson
57 Mrs J. Bailey
58 Mrs Janet Kennedy
59 Andrew Penn
60 Mrs V.J. Mawby
61 Jeremy Cox
62 Ted Geary
63 David Jefferson
64 J. Page
65 Mrs K. Flack
66 Brian North
67 Thames Valley Police
68 Mrs Sheila A. Groves
69 Miss Jill R. Heywood
70 Raymond Hall
71 B. Picknell
72 Chris Ashley
73 James Andrew Baptie
74–78 R. Barker
79 Maria Elizabeth Baptie
80 Martin Bazan
81 Mike Barnett
82–88 Berkshire Library & Information Service
89 T.A. Belcher
90 D.I. Blackman
91 Barbara Bennett
92 P. Bourne
93 Jeanette Brinicombe
94 Ian David Crick
95 Clive Burton
96 Clyde Dallas
97 E. Fellows
98 E.R. Eastbury
99 D.R. Flanagan
100 Nick Franks
101 M.J. Fraser
102 M. Freeman
103 B. Madden
104 Patrick Hayden
105 Pat Harmer
106 Miss M. Henderson
107 Mark Henwood
108 Arthur J. Hoare
109–110 Anne Hunter
111 Philip Ilott
112 David Irwin
113 Ellen Jacobs
114 Paul Graham Joyce
115 R.E. Lewis
116 Peter Mitchell
117 A.M. Reszczyński
118 Matthew James Roberts
119 Robert Edward Smith
120 Jez Strutt
121 David Swanborough
122 John Tennant
123 P.J. Tickner
124 R.M. Wash
125 David Withers
126 A. Abramowicz
127 Tina Marinos
128 Ian Heritage
129 Roger V. Wheeler
130–131 Mrs Stella Skinner
132 David A. Brace
133 J. Cattermole
134 Tracey Howells
135 Sarah Langwith
136 Peggy Clarke
137 D.F. Holt
138 J.M. Sawyer
139 Kevin M. McGarry
140 David N. Ford
141 Mrs P.A. Davidson
142 WPC 113 A.H. McMahon
143 N.J. Shedwood
144 N.B. Wilkinson
145 H.D. Johnson
146 Mrs Beryl Lee
147 Hugh Astor
148 Roger Long
149 Sadie Long
150 Rebecca Long
151 Aran Long
152 Marjie Long
153 Mrs J.V. Cook
154 Mrs J.G. Lippett
155 A.D. Gunner
156 Mrs J.B. Perryman
157 Christopher Griffiths
158 J.S. Mankoo

Remaining names unlisted.